The Rise and Fall of the Peruvian Military Radicals 1968-1976

History: Bloomsbury Academic Collections

This Collection of 23 reissued titles from The Athlone Press and Leicester University Press offers a distinguished selection of titles that showcase the width and breadth of historical study, as well as the interdisciplinary nature of the subject. Crossing over into politics, linguistics, economics, politics, military and maritime history, and science, this Collection encompasses titles on British, European and global subjects from the Early Modern period to the late 20th Century.

The collection is available both in e-book and print versions.

Titles in History are available in the following subsets:

History: British History

History: European History

History: History of Latin America

History: History of Medicine

Other titles available in History: History of Latin America include:

José Martí: Revolutionary Democrat, Ed. by Christopher Abel and Nissa Torrents

British Railways in Argentina 1857-1914: A Case Study of Foreign Investment, Colin M. Lewis

Latin America, Economic Imperialism and the State: The Political Economy of the External Connection from Independence to the Present, Ed. by Christopher Abel and Colin M. Lewis

Government and Society in Colonial Peru: The Intendant System 1784-1814, J. R. Fisher

The Rise and Fall of the Peruvian Military Radicals 1968-1976

George D. E. Philip

History: History of Latin America
BLOOMSBURY ACADEMIC COLLECTIONS

Bloomsbury Academic
An imprint of Bloomsbury Publishing Plc

B L O O M S B U R Y
LONDON • NEW DELHI • NEW YORK • SYDNEY

Bloomsbury Academic
An imprint of Bloomsbury Publishing Plc

50 Bedford Square   1385 Broadway
London   New York
WC1B 3DP   NY 10018
UK   USA

www.bloomsbury.com

BLOOMSBURY and the Diana logo are trademarks of Bloomsbury Publishing Plc

First published in 1978 by The Athlone Press

This edition published by Bloomsbury Academic 2015

© Bloomsbury Publishing Plc 2015

George D. E. Philip has asserted his right under the Copyright, Designs and Patents Act, 1988, to be identified as Author of this work.

All rights reserved. No part of this publication may be reproduced or transmitted in any form or by any means, electronic or mechanical, including photocopying, recording, or any information storage or retrieval system, without prior permission in writing from the publishers.

No responsibility for loss caused to any individual or organization acting on or refraining from action as a result of the material in this publication can be accepted by Bloomsbury or the author.

British Library Cataloguing-in-Publication Data
A catalogue record for this book is available from the British Library.

ISBN: HB: 978-1-4742-4168-7
ePDF: 978-1-4742-4169-4
Set: 978-1-4742-4119-9

Library of Congress Cataloging-in-Publication Data
A catalog record for this book is available from the Library of Congress

Series: Bloomsbury Academic Collections, ISSN 2051-0012

Printed and bound in Great Britain

University of London
Institute of Latin American Studies Monographs

9

The Rise and Fall of the Peruvian Military Radicals
1968–1976

The Rise and Fall of the Peruvian Military Radicals
1968–1976

by

GEORGE D. E. PHILIP

UNIVERSITY OF LONDON
Published for the
Institute of Latin American Studies
THE ATHLONE PRESS
1978

Published by
THE ATHLONE PRESS
UNIVERSITY OF LONDON
at 4 Gower Street, London WC1
*Distributed by Tiptree Book Services Ltd
Tiptree, Essex*

*U.S.A. and Canada
Humanities Press Inc.
New Jersey*

© *University of London* 1978

British Library Cataloguing in Publication Data
Philip, George D E
 The rise and fall of the Peruvian
 military radicals, 1968–1976. – (University
 of London. Institute of Latin American
 Studies. Monographs; 9 ISSN 0076–0846)
 1. Military government – History 2. Peru-
 Politics and government – 1919 –
 I. Title II. Series
 322'.5'0985 JL3424
 ISBN 0 485 17709 9

Printed in Great Britain by
WESTERN PRINTING SERVICES LIMITED
BRISTOL

CONTENTS

Introduction: The Military Government
and its Critics ... 3
   The Left-Wing Interpretation, 4
   The Viewpoint of the Right, 7
   The Viewpoints Compared, 9

I The Course of Peruvian Politics 1948–68 ... 13
   Peruvian Political Forces in 1948, 14
   Economic Changes in Peru 1948–68, 22
   Political Developments 1948–68, 28
     (a) *The Growth of Populism*, 28
     (b) *The Reaction of APRA*, 31
     (c) *The Consequences 1963–7*, 35
     (d) *The Left in Peru*, 38
     (e) *The Military*, 40
   The Crisis 1967–8, 45
   Conclusions, 51

II Peruvian Nationalism and the International
Petroleum Company ... 53
   Peruvian–American Relations 1960–8, 55
   The International Petroleum Company: The Legal Position, 58
   The IPC and Political Values, 60
     (a) *Neoliberal*, 60
     (b) *Nationalist*, 65
   IPC and the Military Coup, 69
   Military Attitudes, 71
   Conclusions, 73

III The Military Government 1968–69; Composition
and Outlook ... 75
   Coup Leaders, 76
     (a) *General Velasco*, 76
     (b) *Velasco's Colonels*, 77
     (c) *General Montagne*, 79
     (d) *General Maldonado*, 80
   The First Military Government: Composition, 82
   Civilian Allies, 85

CONTENTS

Evolution of the Government's Political Base; October 1968 to January 1969, 87
Consolidation; early 1969, 91
Differences within the Military Government, 95
Civilian Attitudes to the Military Government, 96
Conclusions, 97

IV The Velasco Government and the Officer Corps 1969–73   100

Background Features, 100
Political Organization, 102
  (a) *External*, 102
  (b) *Internal*, 103
Military Organization, 109

V Promise and Problems 1969–73   114

The Agrarian Reform, 117
The Industrial Law, 123
Sinamos, 127
Conclusion: The Situation in 1973, 131

VI The Crisis 1973–76   134

The Nationalization of the Press, 137
Social Property, 141
The Politics of Labour and the M.L.R., 142
APRA and the Peruvian Middle Class, 145
The Government's Economic Strategy 1969–74, 146
Military Politics, 150
The End of the 'Revolution', 153

VII Conclusions: The Rise and Fall of the Peruvian Military Radicals   160

Bibliography   168

Index   173

MAPS

1 Peru: Major Towns, 1
2 Peru: Administrative Departments, 2

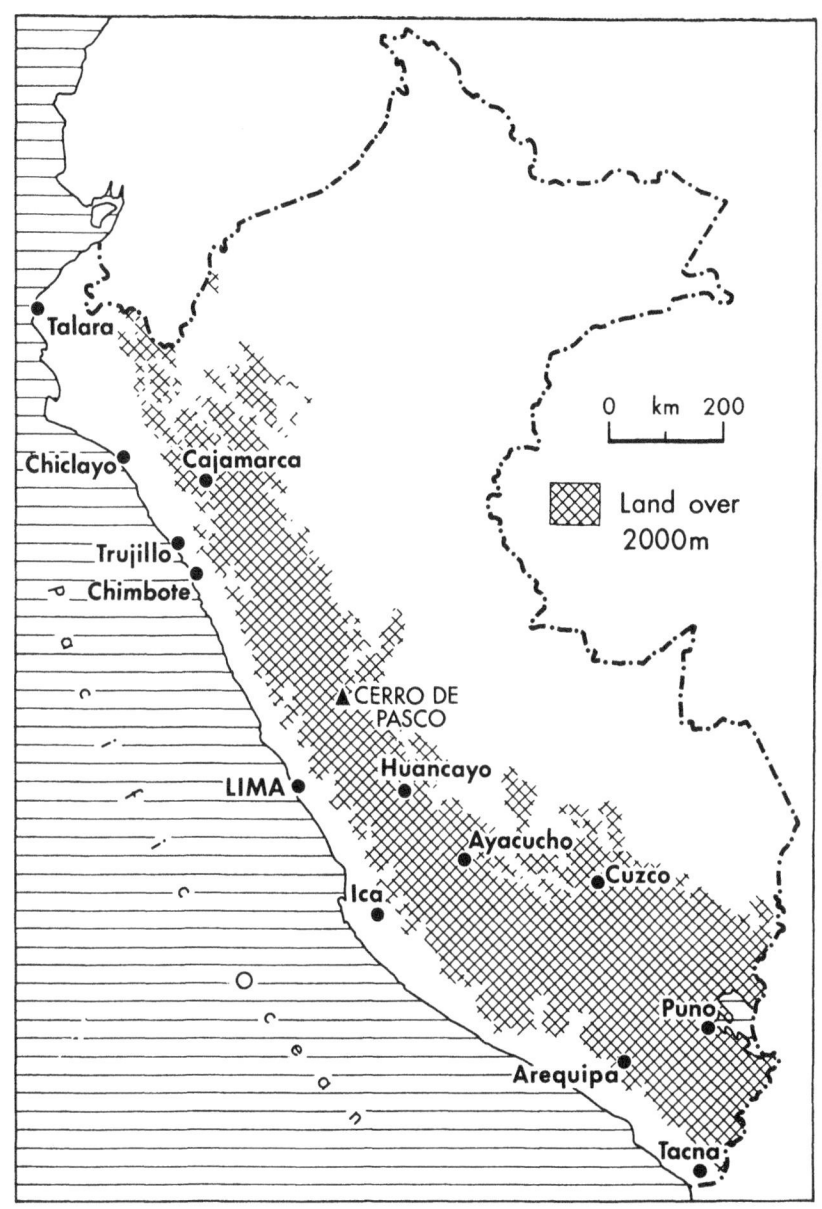

Map 1. Peru: Major Towns

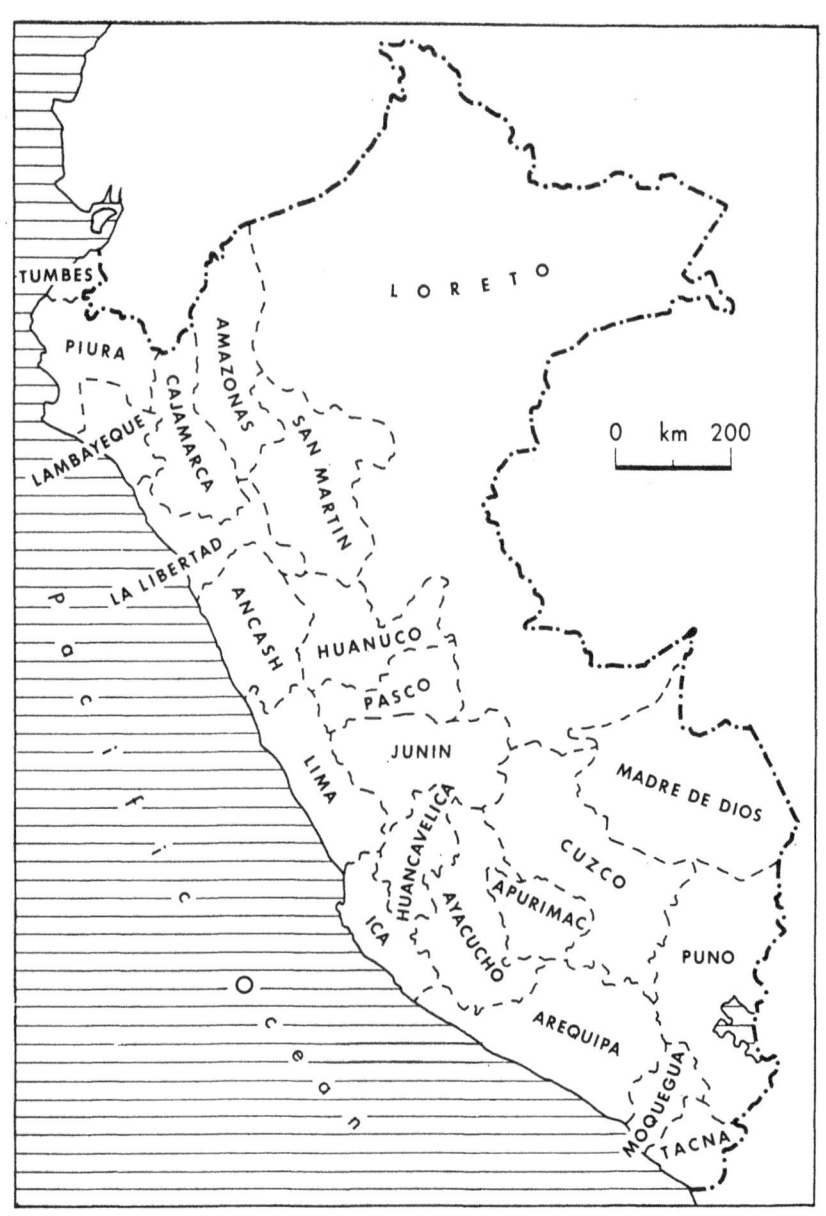

Map 2. Peru: Administrative Departments

INTRODUCTION
THE MILITARY GOVERNMENT AND ITS CRITICS

Until the Peruvian military seized power in October 1968, few people believed that a radical military government could emerge in Latin America; the stereotype of the military conservative was still too strong. Thus at first very little notice of this coup was taken outside Peru itself. When the regime nationalized the American-owned International Petroleum Company, its protestations that this was 'a special case' were widely believed. Gradually, however, opinion changed. In early 1969, the regime stood firm on its refusal to compensate IPC and challenged the American government to cut off aid. Later in that year it decreed, and began to carry out, a radical programme of agrarian reform. This was followed, in 1970, by the nationalization of several banks and a number of mineral deposits, and by an Industrial Law which was greeted with horror by both domestic and foreign capitalists. The Industrial Law, in fact, marked a turning point. Not only did it carry through the regime's intention to nationalize a large part of the economy, but it also sought to encourage worker participation in economic decision-making. Subsequently further legislation was introduced to carry the concept of political and economic 'participation' very much further.

By then observers had begun to revise their judgements about the regime, which had now come to enjoy a good deal of international attention. Even now, however, while the government's actual policies have been widely explored and are fairly well understood,[1] its political dynamics remain bitterly controversial. Indeed, the regime's sudden emergence in 1968, and its

[1] The most comprehensive published works on Peruvian government policy since 1968 are A. Lowenthal, *The Peruvian Experiment; Continuity and Change under Military Rule* (Princeton; 1975), E. V. K. Fitzgerald, *The State and Economic Development; Peru since 1968*; (Cambridge, 1976), and D. Collier, *Squatters and Oligarchs; Authoritarian Rule and Policy Change in Peru* (Baltimore and London, 1976). R. Thorp and G. Bertram's forthcoming *Economic history of Peru since 1890* (Cambridge; printing in 1977) will be up to date and thorough. There is also D. Chaplin, ed.,

almost equally unexpected conservative transformation in 1975-6, provoke several intriguing questions—some very narrowly based and specific, but others as general as the theoretical writing on the politics of Latin America.

It is best to begin by outlining existing treatments of the military government. In order to do this, however, it will be necessary to reduce a voluminous body of writing to manageable proportions, and thus to oversimplify somewhat in presenting particular outlooks. Existing views will be treated, however, not as straw men to be demolished, but rather as expressions of key assumptions which need to be considered along with the subject matter itself.

The Left-Wing Interpretation

In fact the main interpretations of the politics of the regime can be reduced to two general approaches. According to the first, associated with the Left-wing opposition, the military intervened in order to carry out the policies which the civilian 'populist' parties had advocated but been unable to carry through.[2] In this view the coup was the logical conclusion of a process which began with the transformation of the Peruvian economy after around 1950. Before this Peru had been a typical dependent economy, ruled over by an export-oriented oligarchy which was tied closely to foreign interests. Subsequently there had grown up a new set of economic interests, located in the 'modern' sectors of economy (such as manufacturing and fish-

---

Peruvian Nationalism; A Corporatist Revolution (New Jersey, 1976). This is more sociological in tone, but, despite its title, it devotes most of its attention to pre-1968 Peru. So do R. Miller, C. T. Smith and John Fisher in their *Social and Economic Change in Modern Peru* (Liverpool, 1976), although this does contain some interesting data on the military regime. Unpublished doctorates, concentrating on particular sectors, have been written by J. Ballantine, 'The Political Econony of the Peruvian *Gran Mineria*', (Cornell; 1974), and G. Philip, 'Policymaking in the Peruvian Oil Industry, with special reference to the period 1968-73' (Oxford, 1975). A fairly comprehensive bibliography is provided in Lowenthal, op. cit.

[2] The Left-wing opposition made its voice heard by publishing *Sociedad y Politica* when the military government permitted. The leading contributors to this journal, Julio Cotler and Anibal Quijano, have also published elsewhere. See A. Quijano's *Nationalism and Capitalism in Peru* (New York, 1971) and J. Cotler, 'Political Crisis and Military Populism', in *Studies in Comparative International Development*, vol. 6 no. 5 (1970-1), pp. 95-113 and 'The New Mode of Political Domination in Peru', pp. 44-79 of Lowenthal, op. cit.

meal), which challenged the political supremacy of the traditional economic interests but were unable to overcome them. There thus occurred a crisis in Peru, which came about as a result of the new groups' failure to implement the structural reforms (notably of finance and land tenure) that would have made further economic progress possible. This failure was due to the new interests' lack of effective political organization, which resulted from the division of 'populist' forces between two civilian parties—APRA and *Acción Popular*. Thus, when the crisis became acute, the military, representing similar 'populist' (i.e. middle-class) aspirations, intervened in an effort to succeed where their civilian counterparts had failed.

The military programme, therefore, was essentially limited and ultimately pro-capitalist. These limitations were effectively disguised, at first, by the vigour with which the military government pressed the nationalist issue, and by the determination of its attack upon the oligarchy. For a time, therefore, the military could seem to be leading all popular forces (workers and peasants, as well as middle-class groups) against foreign investors and the oligarchy. Inevitably, however, this could not last. The private sector, worried by the government's early reformist measures and uncertain about its ultimate intentions, held back its investment. The government then tried to maintain its radical momentum by expanding the state sector and financing this expansion by (largely foreign) borrowing.

This strategy, however, was doomed to failure. A large public sector led only to a new type of economic dependency. In Quijano's words,

the financial and technological needs of this [state capitalist] type of economy can also allow a close association between state capitalism and international finance capital with the latter remaining in a clear position of power.[3]

In any case state capitalism could not solve all the problems posed by a withdrawal of capital from the private sector without wholesale expropriations and thus a revolutionary transformation of the entire economy.

Because of the financial and technological power which the big private companies were able to mobilize, therefore, the

[3] Quijano, in *Sociedad y Política*, vol. 1, June 1972.

state was forced by the pressure of direct and indirect foreign capital to adopt policies contrary to the interests of the workers. Thus

at the beginning, the regime gained the neutrality, or in some cases even the support, of certain popular sectors, thanks to the nationalist and anti-oligarchic reforms that won for it a certain legitimacy... [however]... The need to come to an arrangement with the imperialist bourgeoisie and to maintain social peace entails the progressive reduction of the military government's margin of autonomy and the wearing away at the foundations of its attempts at class conciliation.[4]

Consequently, the government had to depress expectations by creating corporativist institutions under the misleading title of 'agencies of popular mobilisation'.

It is precisely because of these [economic] constraints that the regime is attempting to maintain social peace through authoritarian–corporative political formations which allow popular pressures to be controlled and a policy of offering minor services to be substituted for the redistribution of income.[5]

The Left-wing opposition, therefore, argued that the logic of its internal choices forced the government to become increasingly authoritarian domestically, and ever more closely linked to external economic and political groups. In fact the early reform measures and the expansive rhetoric only served to increase the subsequent social tensions and thus the repressiveness of the measures which the government would subsequently have to adopt.

According to this view there was created a vicious circle.[6]

[4] F. Portocarrero, in *Sociedad y Politica*, vol. 3, April 1973.
[5] Cotler, in *Sociedad y Politica*, vol. 2. October 1972.
[6] The Left did not regard this circle as vicious for itself, however. On the contrary, it argued that the government, by unleashing demands which it could not meet, would bring about 'the development of a popular mass based revolutionary movement which will confront the so-called Revolutionary Government of the Armed Forces' (p. 78 of Cotler in Lowenthal, *The Peruvian Experiment*). Quijano, on p. 119 of his *Nationalism and Capitalism*, even predicted victory for the Left. Thus, the Left-wing opposition worked hard in the mines and in the rural areas to stimulate intransigent demands that would embarrass the government, and it certainly succeeded in adding to its difficulties. Some of the Left, however, supported the government, and one of the regime's foremost Left-wing supporters defended his position on the grounds that the opposition did not 'understand that the only alternative to the present Revolution is a reactionary, Chilean type military Junta'. (C. Delgado interviewed by the *New York Times*, 15 January 1974).

Because the government stirred up expectations which it was unable to fulfil, it had to repress. However, in repressing, its popularity fell still further and it could therefore even less afford to allow public opinion to be heard. Consequently, the government's political support against opposition from foreign and domestic capital fell off, and it came to lack the political means to resist their pressures. Growing authoritarianism, and a move away from redistributive policies, were opposite sides of the same coin, and both were the consequence of the basic economic decisions which the government made.

To summarize, the Left-opposition regarded the regime as being inherently limited by its unwillingness to move directly to socialist policies and to the politics of mass mobilization. Although the government was able to buy a certain amount of time with its initial reforms, the logic of its political strategy eventually prevailed. The decision to rely on foreign finance for growth, instead of moving directly towards socialism, inevitably inhibited the reformist potential of the government. It was therefore forced into the vicious circle of repressing the people and accommodating the investment community.

The Viewpoint of the Right

The second perspective, associated with the conservative opposition, attributed the 1968 coup primarily to changes which had come about within the military itself. These included the effect of military higher education, an increasingly wide definition of matters involving national security, and the general strengthening of military self-confidence. Confidence, however, was not the same as competence, and did not necessarily contribute towards it. Rather, in this view, it operated like alcohol—increasing the desire but damaging the performance. In Peru this damage occurred in two ways. For one thing, the 'institutional' style of military government (which was closely associated with military radicalism) would inevitably create strains and tensions within the military institutions as a whole, which would in turn ultimately undermine any purely military regime.[7]

[7] Thus, for example, according to Einaudi, 'for the military institutions themselves, the longer-run consequences of any attempt to assert a dominant military

For another, there was the question of political experience. Lacking such experience, the Peruvian officer corps was seduced into following a small group of military radicals whose skill and opportunism enabled them to overcome the naturally conservative orientation of the officer corps. These radicals, also lacking experience, expected far too much from political action and consequently suffered from a certain arrogance. Thus, after having destroyed Peruvian democracy through the seizure of power, they went on to damage its economy through the pursuit of idealistic social reform. Such policies simply proved unworkable, especially when carried out by Generals who expected unquestioning military-style obedience from groups (such as entrepreneurs) who fundamentally could not be coerced unless they were first destroyed.[8] Thus, whereas a conservative military might just have managed to survive, the military radicals opened Pandora's box and ultimately suffered the consequences.

The Right was particularly critical of the regime's early intransigence vis-à-vis domestic and foreign capital. Thus, according to one critic,

Ideologues appear to exaggerate the opportunities open to such a country as Peru to defy the U.S. and to act as though foreign capital was beating at the door, begging to be let in. The reality of our world is very different and the power of the big battalions is, whether we like it or not, considerable.[9]

If the Peruvian government overplayed its hand, its economic objectives could not be achieved.

This problem was especially acute as a result of the divisions within the regime and the consequent contradictions in its

---

role in the search for development are likely to include a return to quarters. The return may come later rather than sooner. But it is inevitable'. L. Einaudi in L. Einaudi and A. Stepan, 'Latin American Institutional Development; Changing Military Perspectives in Peru and Brazil' (Rand Corporation, 1971).

[8] For *Caretas*, which has been one of the regime's foremost critics from the moderate (and pro-democratic) Right, the most objectionable feature of the military government was not any evil intention, but its belief that Peru's difficult problems could be solved by unquestioning command and obedience. Other less sophisticated observers simply argued that the military fell under the spell of General Velasco and a few left-wing civilians and consequently carried out unsound policies. See A. Baella, *El Poder Invisible* (Lima, 1976).

[9] M. Grondona, 'La izquierda militar en la América Latina; los problemas, las tendencias y el futuro de la revolución peruana', in A. Canepa Sardon, *La Revolución Peruana* (Buenos Aires, 1971).

economic programme. Thus the government wanted an adequate rate of economic growth, but this was all-but-impossible as a result of the economic transformation which it also sought. This was so because,

The virus of inefficiency is endemic to Peru, and a particularly virulent variety flourishes in the public sector. To shift the principal responsibility for investment and for the administration of a vast number of concerns to that sector is to court delay, duplication of effort, and the use of political rather than economic criteria for decision-making.[10]

The Right was equally sceptical about the government's participationist policies. In its view, social property and military-led democracy were simply contradictions in terms. Moreover, the military government's desire to please the masses on the basis of unsound political and economic ideas, led it to borrow heavily and to subsidize a wide variety of consumer goods in a way that reflected simple ignorance of economic reality. Reality, however, has a way of making itself felt, and did so, according to this view, in the shape of the economic crisis of 1975–6. Once this took place, the government was at last forced to listen to economic reason and it thus moved sharply to the Right.

The Viewpoints Compared

Between these two views, something of a recognizable picture emerges. This portrays a very ambitious government with strong reformist ideals, which ultimately fell between two stools, since it was able to rely neither on the logic of capitalist orthodoxy nor upon the support of a mobilized populace. However, the differences between these two views cannot be reduced simply to vocabulary and ideological preference, or even to economic analysis. On the contrary, they also include a number of genuinely important differences concerning the politics of the military. These differences can largely be brought out in three questions. To begin with, why did the military intervene in 1968? One view focuses on changes within the Peruvian

[10] R. Clinton, 'The Modernising Military; the case of Peru', in *Inter-American Economic Affairs*, vol. 24 no. 4, 1971, pp. 43–66. In this context see also P. Beltrán, *La Verdadera Realidad Peruana* (Madrid, 1976).

economy and society, while the other concentrates on developments within the military itself. This division corresponds to a major difference within the social science literature on the military; in one view, the military is regarded as similar to other bureaucratic institutions, and is thus believed to have its own institutional outlook and priorities, while, in the other, there is the assumption that 'social forces' broadly determine military behaviour.[11] Clearly, neither view is tenable in its extreme form (since it would be impossible to show conclusively that either set of factors had no importance whatever) but the matter of emphasis is important.

Secondly, could the Peruvian military be regarded as being more or less a homogenous bloc, welded together by a tradition of authority and obedience, and reinforced by the resources of command? Or was it simply a political arena within which rival political groupings competed? Tied in with these questions is the argument about whether a military minority could capture power and use its position to block criticism and protest, or whether the policies of the military government after 1968 need to be explained in broader, more 'structural', terms. Certainly, the fact that coups d'état have taken place against military regimes suggests that the loyalty of the officer corps should never be assumed. However, a military coup is a fairly drastic operation, which it may be difficult to mount against an entrenched military regime, unless circumstances become extreme. Conversely, a number of writers on political organizations have suggested that even a secure leadership cannot always command unconditional obedience on matters of policy.[12] All of this sug-

[11] In the former category is A. Stepan's attempt to compare Peru and Brazil in chapter 2 of his ed. *Authoritarian Brazil* (Yale, 1973) and L. Einaudi in Stepan and Einaudi, 'Latin American Institutional Development...'. V. Villanueva, who is a former army major turned scholar and who has provided some fascinating insights into the Peruvian Army, also leans towards this viewpoint; see V. Villanueva *El CAEM y La Revolución de la Fuerza Armada* (Lima, 1972), *Cien Años del Ejército Peruano; Frustraciones y Cambios* (Lima, 1971) and *Ejército Peruano: del caudillismo anarquico al reformismo militar* (Lima, 1973). In the latter category, there are J. Nun, 'The Middle-Class Military Coup', in C. Veliz, *The Politics of Conformity in Latin America* (Oxford, 1967), and S. P. Huntington, *Political Order in Changing Societies* (Yale, 1968).
[12] The literature on 'bureaucratic politics' is now voluminous but perhaps still the most interesting study of political power in an institutional setting is that of R. Neustadt, *Presidential Power* (New York, 1961). Even extremes of formal authority need not generate unquestioning obedience.

gests that, in any situation, the subjective outlook of the officer corps as a whole will be of crucial importance and will need detailed consideration.[13] At the same time, however, the military tradition of obedience, and the resources open to the top military–political leadership may also be decisive under certain conditions. All of these factors determine the extent to which a military government can combine political security with the determined implementation of controversial policies.

Thirdly, there are a set of questions specifically concerned with the politics of military radicalism. Is such radicalism ever viable, in the sense that it can be made secure and self-sustaining over time? Or is it doomed by the forces which it sets in motion —higher expectations, growing popular demands and unease on the part of the civilian establishment? Much existing writing has assumed, for example, that it is both necessary and almost impossible for a radical military government to initiate a workable system of popular participation and has, therefore, been very sceptical about military radicalism.[14] There is also the question of economic management. On the Right, political radicalism is almost synonymous with economic unsoundness, but there is also a far wider spectrum of opinion which believes that—in contemporary Latin America, as in other dependent economies—it is simply impossible to challenge the existing economic order without far reaching consequences. In this view, the culmination of such a challenge is either revolution or collapse.

These questions must be tackled during the course of any attempt to understand the Peruvian military government. Indeed, they are important both to an understanding of the particular case and to the general study of Latin American politics. In order to approach them, this book will begin with a discussion of the political background to the 1968 coup, and will continue with a fairly detailed description of the coup itself and its immediate aftermath. Subsequently, it will try to account

[13] Detailed studies of this type have been carried out by M. Needler, 'Ecuador, 1963' in W. Andrews and V. Ra'anan Eds. *The Politics of the Coup D'Etat; five case studies*, and by R. Potash, *The Army and Politics in Argentina 1928–45* (Stanford, 1969). Perhaps these writers pay too much attention to essentially personal motivations, but the emphasis is important if only as a corrective.

[14] See especially Huntington, *Political Order*, chapter 4.

both for the regime's early successes and for the subsequent strains and difficulties which culminated in the downfall of the radical officers who had led the 1968 coup. The themes outlined here will then be taken up in the concluding chapter.

I
THE COURSE OF PERUVIAN POLITICS
1948–68

General Manuel Odría's coup d'état of 1948 was enthusiastically greeted by the civilian elite in Lima. His revolt put an end to the uncertain, but mildly reformist, government of Jose Luis Bustamante, and re-emphasized the traditional conservative coalition between army officers and the civilian wealthy. At first, Odría's policies were typically conservative. They combined a fierce repression of the radical Aprista party with liberal economic measures aimed at attracting foreign as well as domestic capital. Thus, the Aprista leader, Victor Raúl Haya de la Torre, spent six years confined to the Colombian embassy, having been refused permission to leave the country and unable even to go near a window for fear of the surrounding marksmen. Meanwhile, the domestic elite, and American oil and mining companies, were preparing to invest heavily under Odría's generous new legislation. The general polarization of political forces, between, on the one hand, the civilian elite, the military and foreign investors, and, on the other, the civilian Left, appeared complete.

Almost exactly twenty years later, another coup took place in Lima. This was also aimed at a weak, but mildly reformist, civilian President, and it again frustrated APRA's hopes of political power. In October 1968, however, the attitude of the military was markedly different. The coup manifesto declared that

Powerful economic forces, both national, and foreign with Peruvian support, being motivated by overwhelming greed, retain political and economic power, and frustrate the popular desire for basic structural reforms ... Our resources have been compromised under conditions of notorious disadvantage to the country, in such a way as to bring about its dependence upon economic power, affront our sovereignty and national dignity, and indefinitely postpone every change that would make it possible for us to overcome our present condition of underdevelopment.[1]

[1] This manifesto is reproduced in several places, including V. Trias, *Fuerzas Armadas y Revolución* (Montevideo, 1971).

This change of orientation was emphasized by the first major step taken by the military government—expropriation of the American-owned oil refinery of Talara. Within four months, the government had completed its nationalization of the International Petroleum Company (a subsidiary of Standard Oil of New Jersey), refused to pay compensation, and challenged the American government to apply sanctions if it dared.

Why had the military broken so emphatically with the civilian Right, and how radical had it really become? These questions can only be tackled after some discussion of the changes that had taken place in Peruvian politics during the twenty years 1948–68. These changes were reflected in the political outlooks both of the military and of the Aprista party, and operated in such a way as to set the scene for that apparently new phenomenon in Latin America—a radical military government.

Peruvian Political Forces in 1948

The main actors in Peruvian politics in the years leading up to 1948 were APRA, the 'oligarchy' and the military. Each of these, in differing ways, represented the modern sector of the Peruvian economy, which included the exporting agricultural *haciendas* (mainly to be found on the North Coast,) the oil and mining industries, and certain manufacturing and service activities in Lima itself. The 'traditional' sector, which covered most of the *Sierra* and which contained well over half of the population of Peru in 1940, had little, if any, significant influence over central decision making.[2] The *Serraño* landlords, it is true, benefited from the strength of conservatives elsewhere in Peru, and could generally rely upon the support of the police and army when any disturbances threatened. However, neither they, nor the peasants, needed to be taken into account by the

---

[2] The 'traditional' label is not intended to denote any historical or present-day isolation from the modern sector or from foreign economies; it is simply used to refer to the level of technology in the economic sector. It is generally true that, in Peru, the highly capitalized and high technology sector of the economy is linked directly with the international economy (either through trade or foreign investment) whereas the 'traditional' sector provides food or low-cost consumer goods for Peruvians. This division—characteristic of all dependent economies—is particularly striking in Peru.

government in Lima. Both political and economic power remained highly concentrated.

In fact, the so-called 'oligarchy'—a group of large coastal landowners and bankers—included the major holders of economic power in Peru.[3] Politically, this acted more or less as a group. It did not control any political party (after the demise of the *civilistas* in the early part of the twentieth century) but it encountered few difficulties in making its voice heard. There were informal contacts, which could easily be arranged by what was a social, as well as an economic elite. There was the press, which was influential among some ordinary voters, but which had its real impact through its influence on the army. There were also the 'national societies'. These were employers' pressure groups organized to integrate sectoral viewpoints, and to advise governments. In a country where independent economic advice was scarce, influence of this kind was a source of real power. Cases can even be found where economic legislation was simply written by the relevant pressure group.[4] Moreover, there was naked wealth; oligarchs could, and did, lend money to governments in return for political protection—a transaction which successive Peruvian governments seemed only too happy to encourage.[5] Above all, however, there was the economy.

---

[3] There has been debate within Peru over the question of whether an oligarchy really existed (and if so, what power it had) or whether it would be better to speak of a rural bourgeoisie. Clearly the question is fraught with ideological implications. This chapter will follow the conventional usage by describing the leading agrarian exporters as the oligarchy, and will take up the question of its real political and economic power in the discussion. The best detailed studies of the oligarchy are those of C. Malplica, *Los Dueños del Perú* (3rd ed. Lima, 1968) and D. Gilbert, 'The Oligarchy and the Old Regime in Peru' (Ph.D., Cornell Univ., 1977). F. Bourricaud (ed.), *La Oligarquía en el Perú* (Lima, 1969) introduces a more general discussion of the topic.

[4] 'The content of the Mining Code was greatly influenced, if not dictated, by the wishes of the Cerro de Pasco Corporation and other members of the *Sociedad de Minería y Petróleos*. Robert Keonig, who had just become President of Cerro in 1950, described the code to me as just what the industry had wanted', pp. 153–4. C. Goodsell, *American Corporations and Peruvian Politics* (Harvard, 1974). The Industrial Law of 1959 appears to have been different only in that this was effectively written by a number of economic interests, see Thorp and Bertram, op. cit.

[5] See P. Klaren, *Modernisation, Dislocation and Aprismo: Origins of the Peruvian Aprista Party 1870–1932* (Austin, Texas, 1973) p. 36. Klaren shows that the Gildemeister interests, in conflict with members of the old coastal rural and small town middle class, were able to win support both of President Pardo and Leguía, despite their differences in outlook, by suitable financial contributions at different times.

Any open attack on the oligarchy would have had serious repercussions on the Peruvian budget and balance of payments. Indeed, President Bustamante's rather half-hearted attempts to limit the power of the exporting interests by means of exchange controls were so unsuccessful that they contributed greatly to the downfall of his government.[6] The experiment was so disastrous that it was another twenty-two years before any subsequent government dared to re-introduce such controls.

Nevertheless, the oligarchy, despite its impressive command of resources was, in one sense, vulnerable. Although many of its members were active in politics, it had no means of directly controlling the government. It could not win elections, since the all-important urban electorate preferred to vote for populist candidates. Even more serious was the fact that, despite its generally successful record in this respect, it could not really be said to control the army. It managed instead by dealing with governments as they existed, rather than by trying to capture power directly. In order to be successful, therefore, it needed at all costs to prevent the formation of a strong and hostile executive. Between 1930 and 1948 it did this by establishing a working relationship with a few key military officers.

The Peruvian army was itself no stranger to politics. As Astiz pointed out,

From 1821, when Peru became independent, until 1968, the presidency (or its equivalent) has been held by seventy-six individuals; fifty of them were military men who led the country for eighty-six years. More than half of the civilians achieved the presidency through the use of force and thus depended upon the military to remain in power. The first civilian president was elected to the post in 1872, but his followers had to defeat a coup led by four brothers, illiterate colonels, who could not bear the sight of a Peruvian president who was not a military man.[7]

Early military interventions appear to have been due largely to the army's concern to protect its privileges, and to defend what increasingly came to be seen as its right to rule. Apart from these strong 'trade union' sentiments, however, the army

---

[6] On this, see R. Hayn, 'Peruvian Exchange Controls 1945–8', in *Inter-American Economic Affairs*, vol. 10 (Spring 1957) pp. 47–70. The matter will also be discussed in Thorp and Bertram, op. cit.

[7] C. Astiz, *Pressure Groups*, p. 131.

could not be regarded as politically united. Indeed, the very nature of its politics made such unity extremely unlikely. No agreement was necessary within the military as a whole before political action was taken. Thus, in order to launch a successful coup d'état, an army General (or Colonel) merely needed to rebel at a time when the rest of the army was unwilling to support the existing government. After a successful coup occurred, the new military President would form his own government. This would often contain key military officers, but did not require the involvement of the army as a whole. For an ambitious officer, therefore, opposition to the President was often extremely tempting (whether or not that President was a military man) and coup attempts, both successful and unsuccessful, were frequent. Almost every Peruvian President has had to govern in the knowledge that highly placed military officers were merely awaiting their opportunity to strike.

This lack of unity, or sense of a military 'institution', made it easier for the oligarchy to influence the outlook of military officers, whether by the cultivation of a powerful individual, or by newspaper campaigns of a kind deliberately intended to reflect military sensibilities. Moreover, influential and well-connected members of the oligarchy were always willing to act as policy advisers to low-born and often ill-educated *caudillos*. Thus, for example, Lt. Col. Luis M. Sánchez Cerro, who led a successful coup in 1930, and who began his Presidency with a distinctly radical outlook, came to rely heavily on oligarchic advisers, and consequently carried out extremely orthodox economic policies, even cutting the budget heavily at a time of economic depression.[8] This political alliance, between the military and the oligarchy, which had not been fully operational prior to 1930, took on real shape as a result of the challenge from a third major political force—the Aprista party.

---

[8] See Thorp and Bertram, op. cit. One contemporary source said that—'the old party of opposition to Leguía . . . namely the *Civilistas* has been working patiently and shrewdly and has succeeded in appropriating Sánchez Cerro who is not unwilling to be appropriated' (U.S. Ambassador Denning, November 1930, quoted in B. W. Loveday, *Sánchez Cerro and Peruvian Politics, 1930–1*, Occasional Paper of Univ. of Glasgow, 1973). Their motives for doing so were made clear by Gustavo Aspillaga; 'above all, he [Sánchez Cerro] has the army, which is essential. It wouldn't be the same with some civilian.' (Quoted in Gilbert, 'The Oligarchy', p. 100.)

APRA appeared at the end of the 1920s, and initially presented itself as a ferociously radical and anti-imperialist party. Thus, its first five-point programme read:

1. Action against Yankee imperialism.
2. The political unity of Latin America.
3. Nationalization of lands and industry.
4. Internationalization of the Panama Canal.
5. Solidarity of all oppressed peoples and classes of the world.[9]

The party was largely based in the North, and drew a great deal of its strength from the reaction against the growth of large-scale plantation agriculture, which ruined many medium-sized farmers and merchants, and created a new kind of rural proletariat. In several regions, APRA combined the support of the 'marginalized' middle-class and emergent voters, by blaming 'imperialism' (in the shape of the Grace and Gildemeister interests) for their common predicament.[10] Thus APRA's leader, Haya de la Torre, asserted, in an early Manifesto, that,

the monopoly that imperialism imposes cannot avoid leading to the destruction, stagnation, or regression of what we generally call the middle class. Thus, just as industrial capitalism . . . proletarianises the petit bourgeoisie, . . . imperialism subjugates and destroys economically the middle classes of the backward countries that it penetrates . . . the first defensive act of our people has to be the nationalisation of our wealth, snatching it from the claws of imperialism.[11]

In general, APRA's electoral strength was based in those areas where economic dislocation had been caused, either directly by foreign interests or by the rising domestic oligarchy. These were to be found in the North—on the coast and in those parts of the Sierra where the plantation owners had extended their interests—and in the central Sierra, where the Cerro de Pasco Corporation (an American-owned copper mining company) was extending and modernizing its holdings. Here,

---

[9] P. Klaren, op. cit., p. 109.
[10] The Grace and Gildemeister companies produced and exported sugar from the *haciendas* of the north coast. In the formation of these *haciendas*, a great deal of damage was done to previous interests—peasants, medium-sized farmers and merchants in certain local towns. The Gildemeister story is the subject of Klaren's book. *Modernisation, dislocation* . . .
[11] Klaren, ibid., pp. 112–13.

APRA benefited both from the dislocation created by the normal processes of capitalist expansion and from the slump of 1929. The latter hit Peru very hard, and its effect was especially marked in the largely foreign-dominated exporting sectors—Cerro de Pasco's workforce, for example, shrunk from 12,858 in 1929 to 5,473 in 1930.[12] In other areas, APRA drew strength from its ability to unify and attract various local dissident groups which had sprung up in the provinces in preceeding years.[13] However, in Lima itself, and in the South of Peru, (where agriculture was left largely undisturbed by large-scale rationalization) APRA has never shown great electoral strength.

The virulence of the rivalry between APRA and the other political groups, as well as the later history of co-operation between APRA and the oligarchy have frequently puzzled observers. Indeed, APRA has been one of the most controversial of all Latin America's political parties, with judgements upon it ranging from the admiring to the openly hostile. It appears, however, that APRA could in many ways be regarded as a 'typical' Latin American populist party, in the sense that it aimed to lead a multi-class alliance in pursuit of a vaguely defined set of reforms.

Thus despite his early radicalism, Haya was a professional politician, and not a man to let doctrine stand in his way to power. In fact, APRA's ideological position has changed a number of times, generally in a conservative direction. Indeed even in his early days there was an undoubted flexibility in Haya's ideological approach[14] and this was to become even more pronounced later.

It appears, therefore, that APRA cannot be distinguished from other 'populist' parties by any greater degree of radicalism that it may have shown. Nor can APRA's ideology be singled

[12] See D. Sulmont, *El Movimiento Obrero en el Perú 1900–56* (Lima, 1975), p. 137.
[13] Work in progress by Fiona Wilson (at the University of Liverpool) on Tarma is interesting in this context, and see also B. Roberts, 'Social History of a Provincial Town; Huancayo', in R. Miller et al., *Social and Economic Change*, pp. 130–92. Roberts, like Klaren, found that, 'APRA's strength was that it was truly a regional party. Its bases were as much in the villages and small towns as in Huancayo [of the Central Sierra] or other labour centres. It attracted people with a variety of occupations; the Aprista-dominated Union Syndical de Junín brought together textile workers, transport workers, small shopkeepers and artisans.' (p. 168). There is, however, still much to be learned about Peruvian political geography.
[14] On this see B. W. Loveday, op. cit.

out as unusual. It was certainly highly abstract, and unclear as to the precise policies that should be implemented. Its somewhat pretentious vagueness, however, had advantages. It perhaps gave 'its followers the feeling that they were participating in a wider intellectual world than that of Peru',[15] while it certainly helped to hold together a fairly diffuse set of supporters and provided a smokescreen behind which Haya, the politician, might easily manoeuvre.

What does seem to have been distinctive about APRA, however, was its early aggressiveness. Perhaps it was only natural that a young and growing party in Peru should follow the patterns of demonstration and street fighting that were set by the mass parties of continental Europe. Moreover, it was not surprising that APRA, which had enrolled such potentially explosive groups as plantation workers,[16] might find it difficult to control its followers and hold them back from acts of violence. However, whatever the motivations of those involved, the intransigence of the Aprista party, and the degree of open political violence and assassination carried out by Apristas, whether or not they were acting under orders from the leadership, was probably the major factor in alienating established political groups. Thus, President Sánchez Cerro was assassinated by an Aprista in 1933, after a previous attempt upon his life had failed. Later, in 1939, a senior army officer, Colonel Morales Bermúdez (the father of the current President of Peru), was assassinated when he was acting as Governor of Trujillo. Most important of all, however, was the murder by an Aprista, in 1935, of Antonio Miró Quesada, the editor of *El Comercio*, together with his wife. Nor did APRA's relationship with the press improve in 1946, when the editor of *La Prensa* was also murdered, and APRA was again held responsible.

The military also had reason to act against APRA. After Lieutenant-Colonel Sánchez Cerro defeated Haya in a possibly fraudulent election in 1931, and APRA responded with street demonstrations and threats of violence, the army was employed to restore 'order'. APRA countered by organizing various risings, and attempted coups, of which there were at least six

[15] A. Hennessy, 'Populism in Latin America', in E. Gellner and E. Ionescu, *Populism* (London, 1969) p. 61.
[16] On whose propensity to violence see Klaren, op. cit., chapter 2.

THE COURSE OF PERUVIAN POLITICS 1948-68 21

between 1930 and 1948.[17] The most violent of these movements was the rebellion at Trujillo, where, in 1932, the military garrison was massacred by Aprista rebels. On retaking the town, the military, in their turn, carried out savage reprisals. The 'Trujillo Massacre' has often been advanced as an explanation for the enduring military hatred of APRA, and it was doubtless important.

Perhaps equally important, however, were memories of the other, less violent, though no more successful, Aprista attempts to destroy its military opponents, often by inciting junior officers to rise against their military superiors. The last of these occurred in 1948, when a group of junior naval officers rose against their superiors in the expectation that their action would be followed by a general revolt. When this failed to materialize, the rising was easily suppressed. Nevertheless, it proved to be a key issue in Gen. Odría's coup of 1948, which was followed by an extreme persecution of APRA and a comprehensive purge of the officer corps.

It would appear, therefore, that it was APRA's aggressiveness, rather than its general ideological position, that accounted for the virulence of anti-Aprista feeling. Although a certain amount of violence was certainly tolerated in Peruvian politics, tolerance did not extend to the murder of Presidents, newspaper editors, army officers, or other members of the elite. Moreover, attempts to encourage junior officers to rise against their military superiors have proved extremely costly to civilian parties in other parts of Latin America where, as in Peru, failure has mobilized the officer corps and led to the taking of savage reprisals. In Peru, this polarization worked to APRA's disadvantage. Not strong enough to win a civil war, APRA forfeited the opportunity of winning power through conciliation and compromise.

There may also have been a cynical motive for later military opposition to APRA. By 1948, even if not before, it had become clear that APRA could not seize power, and that it could, therefore, be suppressed without undue risk. Thus, anti-Aprismo provided a tempting and reasonably safe battle cry for ambitious army officers. Indeed, since APRA no longer posed

[17] V. Villanueva, *Ejercito Peruano* provides a detailed list of military uprisings during the period.

a serious threat, it could be used to advantage by ambitious politicians of all kinds. Whereas one possible road to power was to seek Aprista votes in return for the offer of relatively minor concessions, the other was to adopt a fundamentalist position, in order to repress Apristas, trade unions and personal rivals alike. Both of these strategies were used at different times by army officers, with the result that, by 1948, APRA's chances of achieving presidential power on a radical programme had virtually ended.

In 1948, therefore, politics seemed to have reached a kind of equilibrium. The alliance between the military and the oligarchy seemed to be entrenched. Each appeared to need the other; the military provided immediate political force, while the oligarchy contributed money, status and economic expertise. Thus, apart from a brief interlude between 1945 and 1948, when the army made the mistake of taking too seriously the 'triumph of world democracy', all Peruvian governments between 1930 and 1953 (when Gen. Odría began to cultivate a personal following of his own) could be described as 'military oligarchic'. This did not necessarily mean, however, that they were narrowly reactionary. On the contrary, successive governments were careful to cultivate influential sections of the urban labour force, sometimes securing the support of the Communist Party; they also expanded education and social services, mainly in Lima, so as to win support among the growing urban middle and lower classes.[18] Nevertheless, the underlying motivation of these governments was to face the threat posed by APRA. Moreover, although several attempts were made to reach some kind of compromise, both sides had their hard-liners, and the underlying trend of this period was towards confrontations such as that of October 1948.

Economic Changes in Peru: 1948–68

In 1948, this hostility between APRA and the oligarchy was underpinned by the structure of the Peruvian economy. Economic power in Peru was then relatively homogenous, and largely under national control. Certainly important areas of the econ-

[18] See Sulmont, op. cit., and F. Pike, *The Modern History of Peru* (New York, 1967).

omy were dominated by such large American companies as the Cerro de Pasco Corporation, the International Petroleum Company and W. R. Grace, and, as we have seen, nationalism did at times play a major part in Peruvian politics.

However, the agrarian export plantations of the North Coast (most of which were Peruvian owned) remained basic to Peru's economic strength. It was here that the families of the Peruvian oligarchy—the Gildemeisters, the Prados, the Aspillagas and others had established themselves. It was here, too, that APRA had built up its main support, among the plantation workers and those who felt cheated of their land by the expanding *haciendas*. Thus, the lines of political cleavage were fairly straightforward and based largely on export agriculture. Competition between regions, or between differing industries, had not yet emerged as an important factor in politics.

Table 1: Peruvian exports by value, 1950 and 1967

	1950 US $m.	%		1967 US $m.	%
Cotton	68.0	35.1	Fishmeal	204.0	27.0
Sugar	29.7	15.3	Copper	198.6	26.2
Lead	12.3	6.4	Iron Ore	62.1	8.2
Zinc	10.3	5.3	Cotton	54.8	7.3
Copper	10.2	5.3	Sugar	53.1	7.0
Silver	8.0	4.1	Silver	42.3	5.6
Wool	7.9	4.1	Zinc	35.7	4.7
Fish	5.7	2.9	Lead	30.2	4.0
Total (a)	193.6	100.0		757.0	100.0

(a) includes other items, not specified individually.
Source: Banco Central de Reserva. *Cuentas Nacionales del Perú 1950–67*.

By 1968, however, this pattern had changed significantly. In general, the 'modern' sector of the Peruvian economy had become altogether more diversified, and foreign investment had become even more important. These changes brought about a relative weakening both of the Peruvian economic elite, and of their former enemies, the Aprista party. Thus, whereas in 1950, export agriculture was the major foreign exchange earner for Peru, it had, by 1967, been completely surpassed by mining and fishmeal.

Moreover, as a result of the Mining Law of 1950, the composition of mining investment had also changed considerably. The relative importance of Cerro de Pasco, and the Peruvian mine owners of the central Sierra, declined as a result of the vast new investments which were undertaken in the South of Peru. Marcona began its production of iron ore in 1958, and the Southern Peru Copper Corporation opened the huge Toquepala mine in 1960. These enterprises were capital intensive and highly profitable but little or no domestic economic activity was disrupted by them.[19]

Regionally, and in terms of the economic interests involved, therefore, the political issues raised by this kind of investment were very different from those raised by the foreign investments of the early part of the century. Moreover, these changes in the mining sector increased the extent of foreign ownership in the industry still further. By 1968 this had reached some three-quarters of the gross capital in minerals.[20]

Fishing grew even more rapidly than mining after 1950, and brought about the emergence of a new group of domestic capitalists and workers. Although there had been some rationalization of the industry during the 1960s and a significant increase in the degree of foreign penetration, much of the activity was still on a fairly small scale.[21] Thus, fishmeal provided opportunities for domestic entrepreneurs independent of the oligarchy (which did not participate significantly in either fishmeal or mining), as well as providing an important new political constituency. Moreover, the industry employed directly or in-

[19] According to one economist 'estimates... show that Toquepala earned an after-tax return of around 19 per cent for Southern Peru, whereas Marcona earned about 28 per cent on its iron ore venture. The corresponding figures for U.S. manufacturing investment in Peru stand at about 16 or 17 per cent. Although these estimates are not nearly as high as the figures used by some critics, they indicate that Peru had indeed become an attractive country for foreign investors'. p. 309. S. Hunt, 'Direct Foreign Investment in Peru; New Rules for an Old Game', in A. Lowenthal, *The Peruvian Experiment; Continuity and Change under Military Rule* (Princeton, 1975).

[20] E. V. K. Fitzgerald, *The State and Economic Development; Peru since 1968* (Cambridge, 1975), p. 20.

[21] M. Roemer, *Fishing for Growth* (Harvard, 1970), chapter 5.

directly a workforce of perhaps as many as 40,000 by the mid-1960s grouped at various points along the coast.[22]

A third area where expansion had been extremely rapid was manufacturing. Although this was increasingly capital intensive, as a result of the incentives offered by the 1959 Industrial Promotion Law, it did increase employment opportunities quite significantly. Overall, the share of industry in GNP 'rose from an unusually low 13 per cent in 1950 to over 20 per cent by the 1960s: a remarkable jump.[23] As with fishing and mining, the manufacturing expansion occurred with relatively little involvement by the domestic oligarchy, as foreign companies and new groups of Peruvian entrepreneurs took most of the opportunities offered. Thus,

by 1968, a few oligarchic families... were heavily committed to industry. But most had no industrial interests or only modest ones. The economic pattern established at the turn of the century had not been altered.[24]

Most manufacturing growth took place in Lima, to which increasing quantities of rural migrants were attracted. Thus, the population of Lima rose from 334,000 in 1931, to 540,000 in 1940, 1,492,702 in 1961 and an estimated 2,973,845 in 1972.[25] By the early 1960s, over 15 per cent of Peru's population and over 40 per cent of its electorate was located in Lima. As a consequence of this migration, rapid growth also took place in the service sector, which offered a kind of disguised unemployment to those migrants who could not find industrial work. The rapid growth of these urban sectors provided a new set of opportunities for populist politicians. While these sectors expanded, however, others went into relative decline. One sector where the growth rate had been notably low was that of agriculture. Between 1960 and 1969, for example, the average growth rate of agricultural production (at constant prices) had been 1.5 per cent as against an estimated population growth

[22] Ibid., p. 140.
[23] R. Thorp, 'The Process of Industrialisation in Peru' (mimeo, Oxford, 1975), p. 3.
[24] Gilbert, 'The Oligarchy...', p. 351.
[25] P. Doughty, 'Social Policy and Urban Growth in Lima', pp. 75–111 in D. Chaplin, *Peruvian Nationalism*... On this see also A. Gilbert, *Latin American Development. A geographical perspective* (London, 1974).

rate of 2.9 per cent. Moreover, the volume of sugar and cotton exports actually fell during this period.[26] Whatever the reasons for this, its inevitable consequence was to weaken the economic power of the oligarchy.

Indeed, the economic decline of the oligarchy appears to have been quite general. Not only was it true that it had taken little part in the most rapidly growing sectors of the Peruvian economy and that the importance of Peruvian agriculture was relatively declining, but it was also becoming increasingly apparent that the oligarchy was progressively losing its grip on banking—a sector which had been widely regarded as its stronghold. As late as the mid-1960s, one observer went so far as to say that:

> the oligarchy has more than one string to its bow; not only export agriculture and mining, but also banking and speculation in real estate. It is to be found ensconced in such vantage points of the economy as the credit distribution system.[27]

Banking appeared to be carried out less for direct profit than for its strategic importance in holding together more or less diversified private empires and furthering their interests politically. During the 1960s, however, the position of domestically owned banks declined both relatively and absolutely in the face of foreign competition.[28] Thus, whereas in 1960, 38 per cent of Peru's banking assets were foreign controlled, by 1968 this portion had reached 62 per cent.[29] This was extremely high, even by Latin American standards. This change was almost certainly connected with the rapid growth of foreign investment in manufacturing, although it must also have had a great deal to do with the decadence of a domestic elite that had come to be more concerned with social status and political influence than with profit.

Thus, for example, the Prado family, owners of Banco Popular, one of the largest in Peru, used it deliberately to reinforce their connections with military officers. Thus, they,

---

[26] Banco Central de Reserva, *Cuentas Nacionales del Perú 1960–73* (Lima, 1974), p. 24.

[27] Bourricaud, *Power and Society*, p. 40.

[28] R. Thorp, 'The Expansion of Foreign Ownership in Peru in the 1960s; a Perspective on the Military's Economic Policy' (mimeo, Oxford, 1973).

[29] Ibid., p. 8.

had an extremely liberal loans policy towards military officers. Any officer could walk into the bank and get credit. If he was negligent about paying, there was no pressure from the Banco Popular. Many officers had mortgages from the Prados. Since the bank was tied to an auto importer, it was particularly easy for an officer to purchase and finance a car.[30]

As a result of these and other bad debts, the Prados were in 1968 desperate to find an American buyer who might be prepared to overlook the Bank's many economic weaknesses in return for guaranteed access to a large section of the Peruvian market. When the Velasco regime blocked its sale to a subsidiary of Chase Manhattan in 1970, the whole Prado empire was forced into bankruptcy.

The picture emerges, therefore, of an oligarchy which lost its dynamism before 1968 and which was overtaken in economic importance by a variety of foreign, and even some domestic, interests. This overall retreat was well mirrored by several semi-scandals involving the selling out to foreigners by oligarchic interests in seemingly strong positions.[31] This series of retreats may have been profitable to those directly involved, but could not have reflected much credit on the oligarchy as a whole.

Overall, moreover, the 1948–68 period had seen considerable changes in the patterns of ownership and employment. As a result, the scope for political participation had greatly increased, even though it was still limited. The electorate grew from 350,000 in 1931 to around 2 million in 1962. At the same time, economic interests had become less concentrated, with the result that both APRA and the oligarchy went into political decline. APRA, despite being well-organized, and strong among workers in export agriculture (and also among the miners of the central Sierra and the oil workers of Talara) could not automatically expect support in the Lima *barriadas* or from workers in services or manufacturing. Indeed APRA, despite

[30] Gilbert, 'The Oligarchy...'.
[31] Thus, apart from the case of the Banco Popular, considerable attention was paid to the fact that various domestically owned oil companies—all set up by the Beltrán-Gildemeister partnership—used their Peruvian nationality in order to get preferential terms for offshore concession areas, which they proceeded to sell to foreign companies, possibly at artificially low rates in order to avoid taxation. See C. Malplica, *Los Dueños del Perú* (3rd ed., Lima, 1968) on the oil deal. This transaction was also criticized by *El Comercio* in the early part of 1968, and by *Oiga* (3 November 1968).

strength in a few selected areas (notably the universities and the police force) never dominated Lima, perhaps because the broadly anti-Aprista mass media were relatively more influential in the capital,[32] but even more importantly because, with APRA suppressed, Odría was able to build up his own support in the Lima *barriadas*.[33]

The interests of property owners had also become increasingly fragmented, with foreign companies taking an increasing share of economic activity, and with new domestic wealth owners being increasingly ready to stand aside from the controversial and relatively declining oligarchy. In fact, the relative importance of foreign capital in the Peru of 1968 was very great indeed; in that year, foreigners controlled some three-quarters of mining capital, two-thirds of the sugar refining industry, half of the cotton and wool processing plant, half of the fishing industry, half of the commercial banking sector, and roughly a third of the manufacturing sector—all told, perhaps as much as one-half of the modern sector.[34] Unlike the earlier pattern, however, there was comparatively little overt conflict between foreign investors and the relatively declining domestic elite. As we shall see, the nationalism of the 1960s represented intellectual dissatisfaction with the course of Peruvian development on the part of an aspiring political elite, rather than the outcry of groups who had suffered directly from the process.

Political Developments 1948–68
(A) THE GROWTH OF POPULISM

These economic changes influenced the differing political groups in different ways. They contributed directly to the emergence of a new kind of populist politics, which, in turn, had a profound effect upon the positions of the major participants in the crisis of 1948—APRA, the military and the oligarchy. Most importantly, despite the economic growth in Peru during this period and the great increase in urbanization, political ten-

---

[32] This is suggested by H. Niera whose chapter 'Peru' appears in the Penguin Handbook entitled *The Political Parties of South America* (1973), p. 418.

[33] On this, see D. Collier, *Squatters and Oligarchs; Authoritarian Rule and Policy Change in Peru* (Baltimore, 1976), pp. 59–63.

[34] These figures are provided by Fitzgerald, op. cit., p. 20.

sions generally declined, and the civilian Left became weaker. This general conclusion, which would be surprising both to 'modernization' writers such as Huntington,[35] who expected development to bring about an increase in political tensions, and to those Marxists who identified industrial growth with the emergence of a class-conscious proletariat, is of fundamental importance in explaining the emergence of a radical military government in 1968. Instead of intensifying, and thus reducing the autonomy of the state, political conflict lessened, and thus appeared to increase it. As demands upon the government by organized civilian groups declined in intensity, it became easier for military officers to believe that it was within their power to carry out radical measures without encouraging uncontrollable demands from civilian groups, or losing control of the entire process.

If these developments were so important, however, what brought them about? Briefly, the emergence of new political groups in Peru led existing factors to look for new roles, and thus broke up the previous alignments of forces. The way in which this occurred needs to be discussed.

The rapid expansion of Lima and other urban areas after 1940 did not pass unnoticed among Peruvian politicians. Although some migrants may have taken their political allegiances with them, many did not, and could therefore be enrolled by the new political forces.[36] These newly enfranchised urban voters largely contributed to the breaking of the deadlock between APRA and the oligarchy by allowing new 'populist' groups to emerge. In fact, the first politician to make a determined effort to capture the Lima vote was Odría. Although he seized power in 1948 with the full blessing of the

---

[35] S. P. Huntington, *Political Order in Changing Societies* (Yale, 1968).

[36] There is not a great deal of information on this subject, although Collier, op. cit., S. Powell, 'Political Participation in the Barriadas; A Case Study', in *Comparative Political Studies*, vol. 2 (July, 1969, pp. 195–215,) and F. Bourricaud, *Power and Society* ..., all discuss political attitudes within the *barriadas*, and the conclusion emerges strongly that, where politicization occurs at all, it does so as a result of urban influences. Roberts, op. cit., p. 170, however, sees things differently, and concludes that migrations into Huancayo helped to spread Aprista support from the small and medium farmers into a variety of city occupations. If this insight can be generalized, one would expect that the Lima *barriadas* (which drew migrants from a variety of areas) would be fragmented politically, according to the origins of their members.

Lima elite, Odría later tried to extend his support through a combination of political organization, selective redistribution and public works.[37] In doing so, however, he lost the support of the civilian establishment which had backed him in 1948, as well as that of those army officers who disliked his combination of corruption, deficit spending and repression. It should also be noted that the South (which was the home of Bustamante) had always opposed Odría and Arequipa rioted against him, unsuccessfully in 1950, and again in 1955. On the latter occasion this opposition was supported in Lima and Odría had to organize elections for 1956 in which he had to agree not to be a candidate. Since APRA was also excluded, the political situation seemed to open up. However, Odría's popular support proved surprisingly strong, and after the austerity and high unemployment years of 1957–9 (during Prado's presidency), he was able to capture urban Lima in the elections of 1962, winning support, both among the Lima wealthy and in the *barriadas*.

The most successful populist politician, however, was Fernando Belaúnde, who led the *Acción Popular*. Belaúnde first sprang to political significance in 1956, when he stood as a candidate against Manuel Prado. Prado, a conservative from a traditional landed family, had attracted Aprista support in the 1956 elections in return for a promise to legalize the party. Prado was, in fact, victorious but Belaúnde ran a surprisingly strong second, and was clearly in a good position for the future. A great deal of his appeal lay in his novelty: he was unconnected either with Odría or APRA, and directed his electoral appeal explicitly to those who did not want a return to the polarized politics of the past. Precisely for this reason, Belaúnde's political base was fairly heterogenous. It included some of the 'old right', who disliked both APRA and Odría. This category included the important Lima daily *El Comercio*. Belaúnde also attracted many of the emerging Peruvian capitalists, particularly in the fishmeal sector which felt at home neither with the old landed-banking oligarchy, nor with APRA. These interests were partly reflected by the daily newspaper *Expreso*, whose Editor later became Belaúnde's Minister of Finance. Moreover, Belaúnde attracted many of the Lima poor, who proved sus-

[37] D. Collier, op. cit., pp. 59–63 and D. Sulmont, op. cit., chapter 7.

ceptible to his media-based campaigns and his promise of reform. Subsequently, he also attracted a numerically small, but influential, Left-wing fringe which saw him as their only chance of achieving political prominence. Above all, however, Belaúnde attracted widespread support in the South. He was himself a Southerner, and one, moreover, whose father had earlier been Prime Minister under the last major Southern politician—President Bustamante. Thus, in 1962 and 1963, Belaúnde took over 50 per cent of the vote in both Cuzco and Arequipa.

Belaúnde's own political position was almost classically 'populist'. He said very little about social conflict (apart from the occasional ritual attack on the oligarchy) and emphasized such potentially unifying factors as 'nativism' (he spent a great deal of time in the interior, and was fulsome in his praise of Inca civilization), and 'technical' and 'co-operative' solutions to problems, which he claimed to be able to offer, being himself an architect. His enthusiasm for *co-operación popular*, decentralization, road building and a limited land reform might not have amounted to a coherent programme, but they worked well enough electorally. Belaúnde was broadly pro-American (certainly very much so when it was a question of receiving aid from the American government) but was nevertheless willing to take nationalistic stands on particular issues where he thought that this would help him politically. It says much about the non-revolutionary nature of Peruvian politics that a candidate of this kind could achieve such rapid success. As will be seen, however, this particular combination of attitudes was to lead Belaúnde into trouble during the course of his Presidency.

(B) THE REACTION OF APRA

The existing political actors felt the impact of these new populist forces in different ways. Perhaps the most drastic change came in the outlook of the Aprista party. As we have seen, APRA started its political life on the Left, and earned the bitter enmity of many conservative military officers, as well as the oligarchy. APRA did, in fact, make several efforts to win over military sympathizers, but each time without success. After the fiasco of 1948, however, and the subsequent purge of

Aprista sympathizers in the army, this tactic was abandoned. Instead, APRA began to cultivate the parties of the civilian Right, partly in return for concrete concessions, but largely as a reaction against the rise of Belaúnde.

Although Belaúnde and Haya were never personal friends, personal motivations have rarely been important to APRA.[38] Haya was, after all, willing to do a deal with Odría in 1963, despite the fact that the latter had once made a determined effort to kill him. Probably of more significance, therefore, was the extent of the political threat posed to APRA by Belaúnde. The civilian oligarchy and the army had, it was true, barred APRA from power many times, but they had never tried to undermine its constituency. Haya's main resource, popular support, was safe from them, and it could at least be bartered in return for specific privileges and the hope of eventual tolerance. Belaúnde's challenge, however, was potentially much more deadly. His threat was to deprive Haya of his electoral strength and thus of his political significance. If APRA could not win elections, it really could be ignored. Faced with this populist challenge, Haya could not bring himself to ally with Belaúnde. He preferred instead to deal with those who still needed, or at any rate could still use, his political support; that is to say the oligarchy. Thus, in 1956 Haya, having been forbidden to stand for the Presidency himself, preferred to support Manuel Prado rather than Belaúnde and in 1962, when the Presidential election was deadlocked, he again avoided Belaúnde and preferred to give his support to Odría. Between 1963 and 1968, when Belaúnde was president, APRA joined the Odriístas in opposition to the government and successfully denied it any opportunity of carrying out the reforms to which both parties were theoretically committed.

Thus APRA's move to the Right helped to protect the position of the oligarchy. The civilian Right had no significant electoral support of its own, despite the restricted nature of the

---

[38] Haya undoubtedly regarded Belaúnde as an upstart and once described him as a 'señorito'. The story is also told that Belaúnde sought Aprista support in 1956, but was refused. Undaunted, he ensured that his manifesto was signed by Srs. Seoane, Cox and Townsend (the names of three of the leading Apristas). It transpired, however, that these signatures did not belong to Apristas, but to three otherwise obscure, members of *Acción Popular*. When he heard about this Haya was reported to be furious.

electoral system. The old *civilista* party, which it had once created, was destroyed in the early part of the century and since then civilian conservatives had relied (by and large successfully) on the support of the army. However, the military alliance was not without its problems for them. What would happen if one day a military *caudillo* should decide on economic reform? Colonel Sánchez Cerro had, after all, begun by exhibiting radical tendencies although he was soon tamed. In 1945, moreover, Benavides had antagonized certain oligarchic families by handing over power to Bustamante rather than to one of themselves. Later, General Odría had shown signs of developing a personalist following and had tried to turn the repressive apparatus against the oligarchy itself when the latter had protested. Under him Beltrán, the editor of the conservative *La Prensa*, had been gaoled for nearly a month and the *Club Naciónal*, which was the meeting place of the civilian elite, had been raided by the police.

Thus, the civilian Right had its own reasons for dealing with the Apristas, in order to be released from what might, in time, prove to be an embarrassing dependence on the military. By 1956, there were, in any case, few conflicts of interest between the groups which each side represented. APRA had by this time largely succeeded in unionizing its workers in the major export industries. The Federation of Sugar Workers had been founded in 1945, and

> throughout the post-war years, APRA-controlled unions made significant gains for the mass of sugar workers of the north. Indeed, during this period, most of the pro-labour planks of the early Aprista programme ... were finally achieved. By the late 1960's, the Aprista working class clientele ... had clearly become a select elite within the broad spectrum of the nation's labouring population.[39]

The position of those workers would not necessarily be helped by sweeping land reforms or nationalizations, since these might

---

[39] Klaren, op. cit., p. 154. A similar point is made by Brian Roberts who is concerned with a very different region. 'APRA was a class party, representing the migration and economic diversity of the wider smallholding peasants of the Huancayo area. In this area, APRA never penetrated the poorer peasants who were often the wage labourers of the wider smallholders.' Roberts in R. Miller, op. cit., p. 170.

rouse the expectations of even poorer, and, as yet, unorganized, sections of the community. Moreover, Aprista unions had a great deal to gain from a period of democracy, in which they could organize and operate openly. A secure civilian government, therefore, would have been especially welcome after the repression which APRA had suffered under Odría.

APRA's nationalism had gone the same way as its reformism, and for similar reasons. One example may be used to illustrate the general trend. In 1930, Haya, returning from Europe, landed at Trujillo and

ceremoniously kissed Peruvian soil, and declared to the assembled throng that Talara—dominated as it was by the International Petrol Company—was another 'Canal Zone of Imperialism' which must be revindicated by nationalisation.[40]

In the late 1950s, however, this position was different. From 1945 APRA unionized the workforce, and—after a change in management—IPC's corporate strategy also began to change. Wages and working conditions improved steadily until they came to rank among the best in Peru. In the later years of the IPC controversy, therefore, the APRA-controlled workforce included some of the most outspoken opponents of nationalization, contrasting their own position with the low pay and poor conditions suffered by the workers for the state oil company.

Thus between 1956 and 1962 President Prado, who had been elected with Aprista support, continued to govern with it. He faced no real Aprista pressure to carry out a land reform, or even to depart from economic orthodoxy in the face of domestic recession. In a conservative sense, the Prado government was, in fact, the most successful civilian administration in post-war Peru. It commanded a congressional majority, and was thus able to push through its legislation. It survived, and helped to overcome, a period of severe economic difficulty without falling victim to military intervention. Indeed, it almost completed its entire term of office. Had the results of the 1962 election been more clear cut, President Prado might well have been able to hand over to an elected civilian successor.

These elections, however, did not prove to be clear cut, and their indecisive nature set the stage for another brief military

[40] Ibid., p. 128.

interregnum. In 1962 there were three major candidates, as well as a number of minor ones. None of these, however, was able to secure the necessary one-third of the vote, and the election was then referred to Congress.[41] When faced with a military veto on his own candidacy, Haya offered to support Odría, rather than Belaúnde, in return for a promise of various privileges. This seemingly strange relationship was briefly interrupted by a military coup in June. Elections were scheduled again for July 1963, with Belaúnde clearly the military choice for President. This time he was duly elected, and Haya and Odría joined together in opposition.

(c) THE CONSEQUENCES, 1963-7

In Peru, opposition to civilian government has always been effective when it has controlled Congress. Thus, President Prado was relatively immune from political attack because his Aprista support gave him a Congressional majority. Belaúnde was not so lucky, since his party was outnumbered by the combined strength of APRA and UNO (see Table 2).

Congressional elections in Peru were held at the same time as Presidential ones, so that there was no possibility of a minority President, such as Belaúnde, hoping for better things at some kind of mid-term. However, the powers entrusted to

Table 2: Congressional strength in Peru, after 1963 elections

	Senate	Chamber of Deputies
Acción Popular/Christian Democrats	20	50
APRA	18	58
UNO	7	27
Other	0	5
Total	45	140

· *Source:* Astiz, *Pressure Groups*, p. 103.

[41] Niera, op. cit., lists the 1962 results as follows (main candidates in percentages) Haya de la Torre 32.98 per cent, Belaúnde 31.12 per cent and Odría 28.43 per cent. For 1963, the results were Belaúnde 39.06 per cent, Haya 34.55 per cent and Odría 23.5 per cent.

Congress were considerable. Not only did it need to approve legislation, including the budget, but it was also empowered to censure individual ministers by a majority vote, and thus to force their resignation. Indeed, between 1963 and 1968, the opposition censured ten ministers, and forced them to resign.[42]

Opposition has been a role that Congress has always known how to play. In the early part of the century Congress had systematically delayed agreements with foreign investors which had been submitted by the President.[43] Congress was instrumental in frustrating Bustamante's plan for awarding a concession to IPC for exploration in the Sechura desert. Even during the Odría period, when APRA was suppressed, Congress still modified the proposed Petroleum Law quite substantially. Under Prado, however, Congress was relatively tranquil, since Aprista support was enough to give Prado a congressional majority, but this period was the exception rather than the rule.

After 1963, the opposition majority became very assertive. It modified already weak land-reform legislation, making the financing of expropriation on any large scale impossible, and so turning the law into an instrument for taking the heat out of local protests rather than of carrying out reform in any real sense. It denied Belaúnde taxes, limiting the money which he could spend on his development projects, while at the same time greatly increasing teachers' salaries (since APRA was well represented in the teaching profession). Hunt described the passing of this measure,

Most of this increase [in spending] originated in the now-famous Law 15215 which decreed a 100 per cent increase in all teachers' salaries,

[42] An example of the way in which this power was used can be seen from the censure of the Minister of Government (Interior) in August 1967. A far-Left deputy, Villarán, attended a demonstration to oppose the American presence in Vietnam. This was broken up by the police, who injured him. He went immediately to the Congress building and attacked the government for instituting police repression, and his accusations were supported by the parties of the Right. On the same day, a motion of censure against the Minister responsible for the police was supported by both APRA and the Odriístas, and was passed by both Chambers.

[43] See R. Miller, 'Foreign Firms and the Peruvian Government', in D. C. M Platt (ed.), *Business Imperialism; an analysis based on the British experience in Latin America before 1930* (O.U.P., forthcoming).

to be provided in four annual steps of 25 per cent each, a great expansion of teacher training facilities, and the guarantee of a job with the government for every newly-graduating teacher. This extraordinary law provoked hardly any opposition when it was introduced in Congress in 1964, so eager were all political parties to look good before so large and influential a block of voters, despite the fact that the fiscal planning required for implementing the law was, to say the least, inadequate. Within two years this fiscal commitment among others, provoked an economic crisis from which Peru has not yet fully recovered.[44]

Despite these difficulties Belaúnde went ahead with ambitious spending projects, and in September 1967 was forced into a devaluation of nearly 40 per cent. The immediate political effect of this setback was to increase the assertiveness of Congress, which rejected three post-devaluation budgets. While it was politically conservative, however, the opposition had no hesitation in attacking agreements with foreign companies when it could see political advantage in doing so. The Toquepala contract with the Southern Peru Copper Corporation, and the agreement which Belaúnde reached with ITT, were both attacked as being too friendly to foreign interests.[45]

Thus, the role which Congress played many times in its history was played even more strongly after 1963. The ensuing deadlock increased the opportunities for military intervention, just as it had under Bustamante, and even earlier. As McCoy noted,

Congress is an institution important not only to public policy, but also to the very survival of civilian government. But the Congressional role in both areas is essentially negative.[46]

[44] S. Hunt, 'Distribution, Growth and Government Economic Behaviour in Peru' (Woodrow Wilson School, Princeton Univ. Development Research Program, paper no. 7) p. 30.
[45] On the I.T. and T. contract, see Goodsell, op. cit., chapter 6. The revision of the Toquepala contract is discussed in Hunt (in Lowenthal (ed.), *The Peruvian Experiment* . . .) pp. 307-10, as well as in Malpica, op cit., and J. Ballantine, 'The Political Economy of the Peruvian *Gran Minería*' (Unpublished Ph.D., Cornell Business School, January 1974) chapter 1. Congress also found time to attack the small state-owned oil company EPF, on the grounds that private ownership was intrinsically superior to state control.
[46] T. McCoy, 'Congress, the President and Political Stability in Peru', in W. Agor (ed.), *Legislatures in Latin America; their role and influence* (New York, 1971) p. 353.

This particular difficulty of governing after 1963 might be attributed to the general political fragmentation that took place after 1948, but the institutional dimension is also significant. Opposition was entrenched and, given the existence of a military veto, it did not really expect to be able to take over the Presidency. It therefore determined to make the best use of what it had. This assertion of Congressional power was quite self-conscious. As Haya said,

We did not win control of the Palace, but we did win Congress, and from there we have begun to teach the conception of a new democracy, to endow parliament with an institutional hierarchy. It is parliament that makes the laws that are the norms and base of an organised democracy.[47]

There can be no doubt that Haya, at least, was interested in the obstruction of Belaúnde's proposals primarily in order to show that he still had a power capability. His tactics seemed to be to divide *Acción Popular*. He was well aware that its unity was fragile and the advantages of bringing about such a split would be great.[48] Such an event would force the Right-wing faction, which included Belaúnde himself, to make a further bid for Aprista support from rather a weak bargaining position. In those circumstances, APRA would be in a very strong position to name its candidate for 1969; not, perhaps, Haya himself (who was getting old), but at least a reliable member of a conservative coalition.

(D) THE LEFT IN PERU

The emergence of Belaúnde, and APRA's consequent move to the Right were also of great importance to the civilian Left. Before 1945 the major Left-wing party of Peru was clearly APRA, which combined a radical programme with a mass following. Its only rival in this respect was the small Communist

---

[47] Quoted in ibid., p. 352.
[48] Niera quotes a leading Aprista as saying that *Acción Popular* has 'new style plutocrats side by side with old fashioned leftists', op. cit., p. 438.

A different, but compatible, hypothesis is put forward in P. Kuczynski, *Peruvian Democracy under Economic Stress: An Account of the Belaúnde Administration 1963–1968* (Princeton Univ. Press, 1977). Kuczynski argues that APRA aimed 'to keep the Belaúnde government discredited enough so that an APRA victory would be assured in 1969 but not so much that APRA would inherit a shambles' (pp. 204–5).

party. This, however, was significant only in the South, and even there it was not of great importance. Thus, for a long time, APRA's hegemony over the Left was not seriously challenged.

Around 1960, however, largely as a result of the Cuban Revolution (which was greeted with hostility by Haya), the position of the Left changed considerably. It was not simply that APRA had moved to the Right, but rather that developments appeared to create new options for radical politics. APRA itself, however, was so well organized, and so tightly centralized by this time,[49] that the Left found that it had little chance of exerting any influence within the party. In any case, there appeared to be other possibilities.

One of these was guerrilla warfare, which in Peru (with its unreformed, and backward Sierra) appeared especially promising. Thus, in the late 1950s, Hugo Blanco began organizing peasants in the valley of *La Convención* (in the Southern Sierra) with the very dubious help of the Trotskyist International and the rather inept support of a small group of radicals in Lima.[50] Despite the weakness of his urban support, however, he was able to achieve considerable local success before his arrest in 1963. The main insurgency, however, took place in 1965 and was led by the MIR (which was largely composed of former Apristas who had left that party in 1959). This proved totally unsuccessful, and was easily suppressed by the Peruvian army.

A second option was cultivation of the army itself. The more nationalist members of the civilian Left were greatly encouraged by the military veto of Beltrán's proposed settlement of the IPC dispute in 1960, and tried hard to build on this. Cultivation of the military came to seem especially attractive after the disappointing electoral results of 1962, and, as the 1960s wore on, there were increasing signs that many officers were receptive to radical views. For a time, however, much of the civilian Left was attracted to the third option—supporting the various populist parties which grew up in the mid-1950s. These had programmes which were more or less radical, but competition

---

[49] After its experiences of the early 1930s, when much of the political violence for which APRA was blamed had been unauthorized, Haya had taken care to impose centralized control, even if some local enthusiasm was lost in the process.
[50] On this, see R. Gott, *Rural Guerrillas in Latin America* (London, 1973), pp. 380–90

between them was intense, and all but one of them failed in the 1962 elections. The exception, *Acción Popular*, was the one in which the radical wing, although still substantial, had the least influence. Belaúnde himself, backed by a number of economic interests (notably fishmeal), was quite unwilling to confront either the established economic powers or a hostile, opposition-dominated Congress. Thus, various promised reforms were either postponed or greatly diluted. Nevertheless, Belaúnde's own popularity, and the ambiguity of his intentions, largely protected him against criticisms from the Left of *Acción Popular* during his first three years as President. Moreover, during this time there was at least a vigorous programme of government spending. However, the devaluation, the rigorous spending cuts which followed, and Belaúnde's subsequent overtures to APRA, brought the Left increasingly into opposition.

(E) THE MILITARY

Finally, the military itself underwent major changes in the years after 1948. Although there were many reasons for this, some of the most important were related to the changes which were taking place in the outlook of other political groups. The prospect that a strong and united civilian Right might emerge must have been particularly disturbing, especially to those officers who were serious in their desire for social reform. In any case, the formation of a conservative civilian coalition would make future military intervention more difficult and might even close off the military road to power altogether.

Moreover, APRA's move Right had direct repercussions on the outlook of the officer corps. No longer was it possible, as it had been in 1948, for conservative officers to denounce radical ones as secret Aprista sympathisers, and thus to remove them from positions of influence. Now, radical officers could credibly claim to be the more loyal to the spirit of the institution. They could devotedly serve the military and redefine its objectives. Moreover, APRA's alliance with the oligarchy undoubtedly made many officers feel that they had been used. They had been receptive to propaganda from the oligarchic press about the evils of Aprismo and the need to combat it at all costs, only to find that Prado, Odría, and the other political representatives of the elite were only too happy to rely on Aprista votes when it served their purposes to do so. Finally, more cynical calculations pointed in a similar direction. After APRA's settlement with the oligarchy, something of a political vacuum emerged on the Left. By moving into it, a reformist military government might pick up much of the popular support enjoyed by APRA, and thus destroy its rival once and for all.

There were also other, more 'institutional', reasons for a change in military outlook. Measured by social origin, there had always been a real gulf between military and civilian elites.[51] The main conservatizing influences on the military, therefore, came from outside the army itself. The most notable factors were the independent prestige of particular advisers and newspapers, and the fear of encouraging any kind of popular revolution—a fear that was well expressed by military hostility towards APRA. It was important, therefore, that, just at the time when APRA was moving to the Right, and thus reducing military fears of popular revolution, various organizational changes were taking place within the military which greatly reduced its susceptibility to civilian 'advice'.

The first of these changes occurred with the founding of the military higher education college—Caem. This took place in 1950, partly out of a longstanding commitment to the creation of a Peruvian school of military strategy, and partly to give Odría an opportunity to remove certain officers whom he suspected of Aprista sympathies, but could not dismiss openly.[52] Caem's influence within the military grew only slowly, but by the early 1960s it had become usual for a Colonel to spend a year at Caem before being promoted to General. Although much concerned with purely military matters, Caem increasingly developed social science courses and, in doing so, made a substantial contribution to the creation of a distinctively military ideology.[53] This increased military capacity for independent political action.

[51] This point is discussed again in chapter 4.
[52] See V. Villanueva, *El Caem y La Revolución de la Fuerza Armada*, chapter 1 (Lima, 1972).
[53] The best account of Caem is provided by Villanueva, ibid. See also L. Einaudi, in L. Einaudi and A. Stepan, 'Latin American Institutional Development; changing military perspectives in Peru and Brazil' (Rand Corp., 1971), and also L. Váldez Pallete, 'Antecedentes de la Nueva Orientación de la Fuerza Armada del Perú', in *Aportes*, January 1971.

This is not to say that the development of such an ideology could fully explain the activities of subsequent military governments. Rather, it helped to provide a powerful weapon for the military leadership, and made it easier for future military governments to secure consent among their supporters for the decisions which they decided to take. Indeed, it is generally true that the task of any government in maintaining the allegiance of its supporters is easier if there is a common ideology to which it can convincingly appeal. Furthermore, the content of Caem ideology made it particularly valuable to a military leadership. Caem's most important contribution was to focus on economic development. This was partly due to considerations of total warfare; in any future war, it was seen to be necessary to involve the entire population, and this could only be done if there was a willingness to fight. This willingness would depend upon 'national wellbeing' and could be damaged by extremes of poverty and social injustice. Economic development was subsequently seen as the answer to threats of insurgency by guerrilla movements. French influence at Caem (and so the lessons drawn from Indo-China), the Cuban revolution, and Peru's own guerrilla uprising of 1965 cumulatively created a concern for counter-insurgency which opened the door to a kind of political radicalism.

It would be a mistake to regard this as necessarily a radicalism of the left. Indeed, similar concerns in Brazil led the military government to adopt very different policies. Rather it was a more confident, and urgent, reiteration of what might be called 'traditional' military values, but interpreted in a radically different way. Above all, there was contempt for civilian politicians who were seen as corrupt and incompetent, and unable to solve the problems of the nation.[54] National objectives were defined in a very general way—economic development, wellbeing and modernization. Ideas about how these were to be achieved tended to be borrowed from the parties of the civilian Left. It is also likely that the military was influenced by Ecla's emphasis on technocratic economic management. The rural economy was 'feudal'. Fiscal orthodoxy was not challenged; the main difference from the old conserva-

[54] Villanueva in *El Caem* . . . points out that 'Caem thus *rationalised* the traditional rejection of civilian life by the soldier'. Concluding Sector, emphasis mine.

tives in economic approach was an emphasis on industrialization, planning, and more and better public administration. In fact, the most important feature of Caem ideology was *political* radicalism—a growing feeling that Peru could no longer afford its parties, Congresses and oligarchic pressure groups.[55]

This general military dislike of civilian politicians—common enough among the military in Latin America—came to be reinforced by specific disagreements first with Prado, and later, even more importantly, with Belaúnde.

The first clash after Odría's retirement took place over Caem. Beltrán (Prado's Prime Minister) noticed the growth in Caem's influence, and saw it as a potential preparation for future military governments. Accordingly, he ordered it to change the emphasis of its courses, and cut down on its discussion of political and economic questions. Beltrán also clashed with Caem for another reason. As Einaudi recounts it,

In 1958, the Caem published a proposal for the development of the Central Selva. The study on which the proposal was based was the first systematic military effort to develop cost estimates for a specific development programme. More important, it seriously proposed that a large geographic territory be put under exclusively military administration for the purpose of conducting a controlled experiment in agricultural and industrial development. This proposal was successfully sidetracked by the civilian Prime Minister, Pedro Beltrán, in favour of an A. D. Little research project. Beltrán's innocuous substitute was less dangerous to establish civilian elites, but it earned Beltrán considerable military enmity.[56]

This enmity may have been a factor in the military veto, two years later, of a proposed agreement between the Prado government and the International Petroleum Company, on the grounds that this was damaging to national sovereignty.[57]

The military government of 1962–3, though short-lived, appears to have marked something of a turning point in the outlook of the Peruvian military. Even though the regime did not stay long in power, it did carry out a number of significant

---

[55] One Caem document asserted that 'the sad and desperate truth is that in Peru, the real powers are not the Executive, the Legislative, the Judicial or the Electoral, but the *latifundistas*, the exporters, the bankers and the American investors'. Quoted in Einaudi, op. cit., p. 18.
[56] Ibid., p. 37.
[57] The question of military nationalism is further discussed in the next chapter.

reformist measures—setting up a planning institute, and carrying out a limited land reform in the area of *La Convención*. Most importantly, however, this government found a new way of reconciling its political and military roles and thus sharply reduced what had previously been one of the most important sources of tension within military governments.

Indeed, prior to 1962, military regimes, as such, did not exist. Rather, the leader of a successful coup (in some cases, a fairly junior officer) installed himself as President (sometimes with the help of managed elections) and made his own political appointments. This pattern exacerbated the tension between the military and governmental hierarchies, and thus made military unity extremely difficult to achieve. The system also ensured that the military as a whole would be held responsible for, but would find it very difficult to prevent, the unpopular acts of any military President, with the result that calls for a 'return to barracks' followed almost inevitably after a few years of military rule. The heavy-handed repressiveness of the Odría government, directed first against rioting students, and later against conservative civilian politicians, was particularly resented, and proved extremely damaging to Odría's long-term political ambitions.

The coup of 1962, however, the first since the retirement of Odría, broke with previous traditions by installing a Junta whose President depended upon the support of the three service ministers, whose positions, in turn, were determined by military seniority. Authority, therefore, was vested in the military institutions as a whole and not in any single *caudillo*. Thus, when the Junta's first President, General Godoy, went beyond his mandate, he was removed by his colleagues. Indeed, the new institutional structure made it almost impossible for a coup leader to combine military and electoral politics. Thus, the dismissal of General Godoy was almost certainly due to his efforts to get Aprista and Odriísta support for a candidacy of his own.[58]

[58] He did this by trying to persuade the latter that they had no chance of victory and the former that they would not be allowed to take office even if they won. On Godoy's ambitions, see V. Villanueva, *Un Año Bajo el Sable* (Lima, 1963), pp. 112–15, and D. Collier, op. cit., p. 88. Apart from Villanueva, a good general account of the 1962–3 period is provided by A. Payne, *The Peruvian Coup D'Etat of 1962; The Overthrow of Manuel Prado* (Washington D.C., 1968), and see also chapter 5 of C. Astiz, *Pressure Groups* . . .

A major consequence of this change was to close off the officer corps to a variety of civilian influences. In fact, there were powerful voices within the 1962–3 military government calling for an indefinite postponement of elections while the military itself carried out a reform programme of its own. These views, however, did not prevail. Certain officers may have been influenced by the attitude of the American government which, at that time, was outspokenly hostile to military dictatorships, while others may have had vivid memories of military rule under Odría, whom they did not wish to emulate. Perhaps most important, however, it is unlikely that a reformist consensus yet existed, and fear of Left-wing militancy was probably still too strong to permit any radical new departures.[59]

The military as a whole, therefore, preferred to organize elections in which their preferred candidate—Belaúnde—could be expected to win. Initially, there was a good deal of support for Belaúnde within the military. He was a non-Aprista civilian with a genuine popular base and vaguely reformist aspirations, who made a conscious effort to de-emphasize and reduce social conflict. This support soon began to evaporate, however, when the military had to evaluate Belaúnde's performance in office. His inability to carry out reforms, or even to manage the economy effectively, confirmed the suspicions of many officers that real power lay outside the political arena. Moreover, Belaúnde's unwillingness to rely more heavily upon the support of the army when confronting Congress encouraged suspicions that he was not serious about his reformism, and a feeling that he needed to be replaced by a president who was.

The Crisis, 1967–8

The political effects of all these changes took a long time to work themselves through. The dissolution of the 'old politics' which had seen entrenched hostility between, on the one hand, the military and the oligarchy and, on the other, APRA, was substantially completed by the mid-1960s. The emergence of the new groups generally reduced political tensions by inducing

[59] The Cuban Revolution, and the activities of Hugo Blanco, ensured that fears of Castro-inspired insurgency partially (and temporarily) replaced fears of Aprista radicalism. The question of military ideology will be taken up in the next chapter.

the older political actors to seek new partners, and thus to retreat from their previous intransigence. At the same time, it was not yet clear what new patterns would be formed. In the short-term, the new tentative political alliances that were established simply led to *impasse*. The APRA/UNO coalition had proved strong enough to block reformist legislation but had little prospect of power for itself. The military, still rethinking its position after its experiences under Odría, was temporarily unwilling to take over the government itself, but still refused to allow APRA to do so. Belaúnde, by far the most successful of the populist politicians, was still not strong enough to govern effectively without winning over some powerful ally. As President, however, he still had the initiative. Any choice which he made would be decisive for the future course of Peruvian politics. If he allied himself successfully with the military radicals, he would need to carry out a fairly wide range of reforms in order to maintain their confidence. Any long-term alliance with APRA, however, would provide *Acción Popular* with the civilian votes necessary to maintain an essentially conservative development strategy.

After the devaluation of September 1967, choice could not be postponed indefinitely. It had become clear that Belaúnde's original programme would not be carried out due to the weakness of his political base. Indeed, unless some understanding could be reached with another party, Belaúnde's government would not even be able to resolve the economic crisis. On the other hand, Belaúnde did have resources of his own; elections were due in 1969, and, as various parties jockeyed for advantage, past political alignments might be expected to dissolve in such a way as to provide opportunities for an incumbent President.

From these developments, there were two interacting consequences. First, military intervention, more or less discounted between 1963 and 1967, became increasingly likely and feared (or hoped for). This prospect was particularly worrying to the Aprista party, even though military relations with APRA had clearly improved somewhat by 1968.[60] Secondly, Belaúnde

[60] Thus, at an Aprista meeting in February 1968, five retired generals mounted the rostrum, and the retired army officers' association sent a message of approval. See *Latin America*, 1 March 1968. One should also remember the remark made by General Doíg Sánchez in March 1968 that the army had 'erased the word "veto"

finally made his decision to seek an alliance with the Apristas, and, in doing so, he managed to retain the support of a large majority of his Congressional supporters. These were worried by the declining level of popular support for the party, which had been reflected in a decisive defeat in a Lima by-election, held in November 1967. In this situation, the Right wing of the government might have been only too happy to be rid of the embarrassing commitments insisted upon by the Left-wing of the party.

The Apristas could guarantee a Congressional majority and a substantial share of the popular vote in the 1969 elections.[61] However, they were themselves afraid of a military coup, and hopeful of securing *Populista* support for themselves. It was never entirely clear whether an electoral alliance would in fact have materialized, but the developing AP/APRA understanding did provide Belaúnde with an effective Congressional majority from about May 1968. The most important result of this new understanding came at the end of June when Congress gave Belaúnde sixty days of emergency powers in order to deal with the economic crisis. By this means it was agreed that the government would take the necessary but unpopular post-devaluation stabilization measures, while APRA avoided the direct responsibilities and gained some of the benefits.

from its dictionary'. This ambiguous, but possibly important statement, was made in return for APRA's agreement to stop investigating a naval smuggling scandal. However, it is not clear that Gen. Doíg either wished, or was in a position to, guarantee APRA's electoral security. Indeed, Zimmermann suggests that General Doíg's remarks only stimulated preparations for the coup, which had already begun with conversation between Velasco and three Colonels in the intelligence services. (See A. Zimmermann, *El Plan Inca: Objectivo Revolución Peruano* (Lima, 1974).) Certainly, eight years later, Vargas Haya, a prominent Aprista, claimed that he had got hold of a secret document in early 1968 which had been issued by the military intelligence service (from which many of the military radicals were later to spring). This called for intervention against APRA as a result of the latter party's 'attempt to discredit their adversaries, principally the Armed Forces' through the smuggling investigation. See Vargas Haya, *Contrabando* (Lima, 1976), pp. 155–6. If true, however, this story also suggests that APRA had some valuable connexions within the army.

[61] Another development in 1967–8 of which the effect was not immediately apparent, was the growth of Aprista support among the Lima middle class. One example of this was that Chirinos Soto, who stood for the Senate in the Lima by-election of 1967 on an independent Conservative ticket, followed up his victory by joining APRA. With Odría in personal and political decline, it is easy to see why this choice was made.

Belaúnde's growing *rapprochement* with APRA coincided with his growing estrangement from his own Left wing. The Left, which had never been very happy with Belaúnde's government, became increasingly restive as it became obvious that virtually all of its reform programme was doomed by Congressional opposition, and that the government was unwilling to press the issue. The split in *Acción Popular* was delayed by Belaúnde's appointment of Seoane—the leading *Populista* radical—as Prime Minister in September 1967. However, Seoane resigned in November, unhappy both with the opposition of Congress and the lukewarm support given to him by Belaúnde himself. From then on, *Acción Popular* slowly but steadily broke up.

At the same time, the *Populista* Left was joined in opposition by the nationalist and anti-Aprista Right, including *El Comercio*, whose opposition to Belaúnde stemmed both from his overtures to APRA and his unwillingness to take a hard line in Peru's dispute with the International Petroleum Company. Moreover, although many Odriistas were willing to support an AP/APRA coalition, certain established families were horrified when they considered the tax increases that would be necessary if spending on roads, health and education was to be maintained, and the urban middle-classes thus kept satisfied. The economic 'stabilization measures' taken by Belaúnde's finance minister Ulloa during the 90-day emergency period were particularly resented, including as they did prohibitive tariffs against the import of luxury consumer goods. Thus, in mid-1968, the Odriista party also broke up, with one section looking for some accommodation with the AP/APRA majority, and the other section remaining independent and isolated.

Neither of these opposition groups, however, could have any confidence in electoral success. The far-Right had never shown much electoral strength and had always been able to rely on supporters in the military, or on an understanding with APRA. Now that it appeared that the APRA-oligarchic alliance was breaking up, certain well-connected families again looked to the army for support. Nor could the Left expect very much in 1969. Belaúnde and Haya between them controlled most of the organized political machinery, and could command a significant following in every region of Peru. When, in 1962, the Left had stood against Belaúnde, it had failed miserably. Prospects had

THE COURSE OF PERUVIAN POLITICS 1948-68   49

improved somewhat since then, but not decisively so, and the Left could not expect to defeat any moderate or conservative candidate who had Aprista or *Populista* backing. Consequently, from around the middle of 1968, the *Populista* Left joined the *Social Progresistas* in pressing for military intervention.

Around the middle of 1968, therefore, the long period of political impasse came to an end, and there appeared in its place a clear choice between two very different possible kinds of government. On one side, there were the major civilian political parties and their allies. These had two major interests in common; both wanted regular elections, and both were willing to tolerate a limited degree of economic reform (of land-tenure or taxation) but only so long as nothing drastic was involved.

In fact, no populist civilian government could have been expected to bring about any kind of far-reaching economic transformation. Neither *Acción Popular* nor APRA was opposed to foreign investment, except occasionally for tactical reasons, or in order to bargain for better terms. It was unlikely that either of them would have supported the development of a large public enterprise sector, such as would be necessary if a more nationalist strategy was to be pursued. Moreover, these parties would have had political difficulty in pressing for any genuinely radical land reform. APRA's unionized plantation workers, and *Acción Popular*'s urban supporters would not tolerate anything expensive or disorganized or destabilizing. Thus, neither party had shown any interest in enrolling the rural poor and both had shown themselves willing to repress any radical organization that might appear in the countryside.[62] Indeed, even when such groups were enrolled, there was no guarantee that they would be effectively represented.[63] It is more likely that

[62] See J. Cotler, 'The Mechanics of Internal Domination and Social Change in Peru', pp. 35-75 in D. Chaplin (ed.), *Peruvian Nationalism* and H. Handelsman, *Struggle in the Andes* (Austin, Texas, 1975). According to Handelsman (p. 117) during the repression of a radical peasant organization in the southern Sierra during Belaúnde's presidency, 'an estimated three hundred peasants were killed'. APRA attacked the government for not having been repressive enough.

[63] See Handelsman, ibid., on the role of the Aprista peasant organization FENCAP. Moreover, one study of housing policy in Ica concluded that 'the people of the *barriadas* were mobilised for political power in 1960 by their own Aprista leaders and those from the middle class, but by 1966, although Apristas dominated the politics of the city and controlled the development corporation,

an AP/APRA government would have concentrated more on 'infrastructural' spending, especially in areas such as education where economic justification, and World Bank loans could be reconciled with the creation of a middle class clientele.

Whatever its logic on a long term basis, however, there were serious short-term problems with the establishment of any coalition of this kind. The most obviously excluded group—the military—could not be relied on to make a dignified withdrawal. Moreover, if the army wanted to intervene, there would be no shortage of justifications to enable it to do so. If the motivation to intervene existed, occasion for intervention might be found in some short-term crisis, whether over dealings with foreign companies, allegations of electoral fraud, outbreaks of rural or urban violence, indications of economic difficulty, or any one of a number of other issues.

Indeed, it was the military which provided the other political option which Peru faced in mid-1968. The military faced no immediate problems over taking over power, but in order to act effectively it needed to devise a longer-term political strategy, which could provide the necessary unity for action now that the old anti-Aprista and pro-oligarchic motivations had ceased to be relevant. Certainly, there was no longer any point in taking power for a short period, calling elections and subsequently returning to barracks. Moreover, a purely conservative government would be unlikely to prosper in the face of opposition from most of the middle class and some of the traditional elite, especially since there would be no obvious justification for its existence. Thus, if the military was to govern against the opposition of the major political parties and their supporters, it would require some positive rationale to justify taking power and to shape its policies once it had become the government. The rationale which it did choose was that of nationalism and the way in which it did so will be the subject of the next chapter.

---

not one house had been constructed in the *barriadas*. Middle class Apristas, together with Belaúndistas, representing the new and old financial elites, have used the state institutions to serve their own ends and increased their relative share of the wealth by controlling state funds', p. 238. D. L. Bayer, 'Urban Peru: Political Action as a Sellout', pp. 226–38 of D. Chaplin, *Peruvian Nationalism* . . . (The author was a Peace Corps volunteer in Ica at the time.)

Conclusions

We have already seen that two broad explanations have been offered as to why a radical military government took power in October 1968—one of these concerned the failure of 'middle-class' populist politicians, and the other examined changes in military 'outlook', 'self-image', and 'threat perceptions'. It is clear that both of these contain a limited amount of truth, although neither of them relates to one particularly striking feature of pre-1968 Peruvian politics—the inverse relationship between economic growth and radical political mobilization. Nearly all theories of 'political development', whether 'pluralist' or Marxist, would agree that in a country where manufacturing employment, urbanization, and the size of the electorate were all growing rapidly, political tensions could be expected to increase. In Peru, however, despite all of these changes, political tensions actually declined. Thus, whereas theorists of the military have generally expected that 'modernization', by increasing political tensions, would force the military to take a conservative direction[64] the Peruvian case neatly reversed this causality. 'Modernization', by reducing political tensions, made military radicalism possible. The reasons why it did so are best examined historically.

The first mushrooming of political participation in Peru took place during the 1920s, in the face of economic decline in particular regions, and growing governmental reliance on foreign borrowing and investment. Once the depression struck, it was almost inevitable that this decline would be expressed in radical politics, and, indeed, the Aprista party harnessed the support of a broad coalition of dissident groups. APRA's early radicalism and violence, however, led to a successful reaction on the part of the traditional civilian elite and the military, with the consequence that Peruvian politics became polarized at a fairly 'early' stage of development. Polarization occurred, however, not as a result of economic growth and 'modernization' but because of the severe economic setbacks of the 1920s and early 1930s.

When, after 1948, rapid economic growth once again took place in Peru, the new groups that thus emerged upset the

[64] See especially Huntington, *Political Order* . . . , chapter 4.

previous pattern of polarization and forced the older political actors to look for new roles. The result was that two previously bitter enemies—APRA and the oligarchy—arrived at a *modus vivendi* which freed the military from its previous political orientation, and at the same time, proved strong enough to frustrate Belaúnde's new populism. The APRA–oligarchic alliance, therefore, increased both military motivations to act and their opportunity to do so. With APRA and the oligarchy both discredited by alliance with each other (and for various other reasons as well), and with no new party able to break the deadlock thus created, the time seemed right for the intervention of the radical army officers whose solution to the problem was to destroy the oligarchy and thus try to replace the existing, but failed, populist parties. The belated AP/Aprista alliance, by raising the possibility that a strong 'middle-class' civilian political party might at last emerge, only made military intervention more urgent for those who had already decided to tackle Peru's problems by means of a military-led process of social transformation.

11

PERUVIAN NATIONALISM AND THE INTERNATIONAL PETROLEUM COMPANY

'Nationalism' covers a variety of political attitudes, and can be expressed in many different contexts. Indeed, according to the definition adopted, it can refer to a demand either for political independence according to criteria of language or race, or for military conquest on the same basis; it can even refer to the adoption of various 'protectionist' economic measures, which aim to discriminate against foreign companies or countries. Such different forms of nationalism all represent political demands made by or on behalf of an actual or potential nation state, but they do not necessarily have a great deal more than this in common.[1] In Latin American politics, however, nationalism is usually more specifically defined as hostility towards foreign investment, although even this can take many forms and express many different interests. Even if it is true, therefore, that the military coup of 1968 was 'nationalist', a great deal of further explanation is necessary as to military motivations and ideological attitudes. Some of these were clearly short-term and opportunistic; by mid-1968, the International Petroleum Company had clearly come to present a tempting target for military intervention. Nevertheless, the coherence of the military government's strategy since 1968 suggests that military nationalism was based on rather more than a dislike of vanishing pages in a contract, or a disputed interpretation of nineteenth-century economic history.

At a sociological level, military nationalism was very different from the kind which APRA had shown in the 1930s. As we have seen, Aprista nationalism was largely a response by 'marginalized' middle and working class groups to the disturbances brought about by the rapid expansion of large foreign or

---

[1] A general discussion of political nationalism is provided by K. Minogue, *Nationalism* (London, 1967). Different accounts of particular (non-economic) nationalisms are provided by E. Kedourie, *Nationalism* (London, 1960) and ed. *Nationalism in Asia and Africa* (London, 1971).

semi-foreign companies. It was, thus, a protest against catastrophic (even if 'efficient') economic change, introduced into Peru by foreigners, or by those who could be labelled as foreigners. Once these formerly-marginalized groups had come to terms with the new system, and even created privileged positions for themselves within it, Aprista nationalism became increasingly muted.

Military nationalism was far more 'ideological' and had little to do with any direct losses suffered by specific Peruvian interests at the hands of encroaching foreigners. It can be attributed, rather, to a more general discontent with the way in which the Peruvian economy was evolving. Nationalism, even in the sense of opposition to the International Petroleum Company, was never a major popular issue in Peru; as we have seen, such pro-American politicians as Belaúnde, Haya and Odría dominated electoral politics, and seemed likely to continue to do so. Moreover, there were no powerful 'nationalist' economic interests in the Peru of 1968; there was some demand for tighter control over foreign investment in banking, but foreign capital was generally welcomed in mining, oil and manufacturing. Indeed, it is significant that the most influential and consistent opponent of IPC—the outspokenly nationalist newspaper, *El Comercio*—was the only Lima daily not to be tied to some powerful private empire. Similarly, only within the ranks of the officer corps, where economic interests were not felt directly, could widespread support be found for economic nationalism.

It may seem surprising, indeed, that such nationalism could emerge at all. If it was not based on popular pressure, or on economic interest, then what kind of movement was it? It may be most useful to start by considering the intellectual climate of the period, before going on to discuss the more specifically political role of nationalism and the IPC controversy.

In Latin America as a whole, the intellectual climate moved increasingly to the Left in the course of the 1960s; there was a change from extolling the benefits of foreign aid, investment and technology to pointing out the dangers. No doubt in reaction to the Cuban Revolution, the early failures of the Alliance for Progress, and the growing polarization of politics in Brazil, there came to be an increasing emphasis on the difficulties of 'technocratic' solutions to problems, and the need for fundamental social changes. In the eyes of a growing number of Latin American intellectuals, foreign interests and their perceived connections with a local 'oligarchy' or 'comprador-bourgeoisie' replaced alleged shortages of capital, entrepreneurial skill or technology as the major cause of underdevelopment. This change, when combined with developments which were specific to Peru, undoubtedly help to explain the differences in outlook between the pro-American government of Belaúnde, and the nationalism of General Velasco.

Peruvian-American Relations, 1960–8

At a more political level, the attractiveness of anti-American nationalism became increasingly apparent to the Peruvian military during the 1960s, largely because of a cumulation of irritations. Some minor conflicts between Peru and the USA were almost inevitable in view of the importance of American markets, technology and finance to the Peruvian economy. These conflicts became more intense, however, as after the beginning of the 1960s American policy towards Peru became increasingly activist and—to those on the wrong side—meddlesome. As Einaudi summarized the change,

Until the 1960's . . . given the fact of U.S. power and the profits of being associated with it, most Peruvian officers considered their relationship to the United States, while unsatisfactory, still about the best attainable under the circumstances. Although verbally they often supported nationalist claims against certain U.S. interests . . . the military as a whole did so rather mechanically, more in defence to ultimate ideals than in hopes of their immediate realisation . . . Since the mid-1960's, however, [events] have led most officers, particularly in the army, to downgrade the importance of relations with the outside world, including the United States, in favour of tightened nationalist efforts at military directed self-help.[2]

The first major blow to traditional Peruvian-American relations occurred in 1962, when Washington severed diplomatic relations with Lima after the Peruvian military coup, partly out of anger at what was seen as an anti-Aprista move,

[2] Einaudi, 'Changing Perspectives . . .', p. 20.

and partly as an attempt to deter military coups elsewhere in Latin America.[3] It is clear that the military government was surprised and angered by the American government's decision, but it nevertheless stood firm and Washington was eventually forced to back down and recognize the regime. It may be that, after this, the credibility of American threats to Peru was somewhat reduced in the eyes of the military.

Further strains between the two countries occurred during the course of Belaúnde's government. Between 1964 and 1966, the American government cut off aid to Belaúnde, as a result of his inability to settle the IPC dispute. The object of this measure was to pressure Belaúnde into reaching a settlement with the company, which Washington believed was within his power to do. Goodwin quoted one official as saying,

> The idea was to put on a freeze, talk about red tape and bureaucracy, and they'd soon get the message. Unfortunately, they believed we were as inefficient as we said, and it took about a year for them to get the message.[4]

Severance of aid damaged Belaúnde's already limited chances of carrying out his ambitious spending plans without raising taxes, or otherwise having to deal with Congress. It also helped to discredit the then prevalent idea that economic development could be brought about in Peru at little social cost but with generous contributions from the American Treasury.

Problems of a different kind occurred in 1965, when the army was called out to defeat a rural guerrilla movement in the Peruvian Andes. The American government, instead of supplying or training the Peruvian military as a whole, created a separate army unit to deal with counter-insurgency (on lines similar to those of the Bolivian Rangers). This specialized unit quickly became unpopular with the rest of the military and

---

[3] G. Treverton, 'U.S. Foreign Policymaking in the IPC case' (mimeo, Washington D.C., September 1974). In 1962 American commitment to the Alliance for Progress ideology (which declared itself opposed to military intervention) was still strong, although it weakened somewhat after the Peruvian experience. Moreover, as Treverton points out, American policy had—ever since 1945—been pro-Aprista, and this orientation has continued to influence the American State Department.

[4] R. Goodwin, 'Letter from Peru', *New Yorker*, 17 May 1969. Treverton, op. cit., points out this was not the first time that the American government overestimated its own influence in Peru—nor would it be the last.

with the government, and was disbanded prior to 1968.[5] A related conflict reportedly took place when the American government refused to supply the Peruvian army with napalm, thus 'forcing' it to turn for supplies to the hated IPC.[6]

Aid to Belaúnde was, in fact, resumed in 1966, after a change in the personnel of the U.S. State Department, and after Belaúnde had given assurances that he would not expropriate IPC. A year later, however, relations worsened further as a result of a dispute over weapons supply. This occurred when Belaúnde, in a position of considerable political weakness after the devaluation of 1967, agreed to order supersonic aircraft for his air force. The American government refused to sell planes to Peru, on the grounds that they were too expensive, and that their purchase might set off a new arms race in Latin America. Angered, the Peruvian government bought even more expensive French Mirages, and the USA cut off aid in retaliation. This action was particularly important. It was public, and aimed at the military, whose enmity was already ominous. Moreover, it was something of a last straw for many pro-*Alianza* technocrats. Thus, Levingstone and Onis quoted a 'Peruvian official' as saying,

We have no illusions. We have received little, and we will receive little. First IPC, then fiscal irresponsibility, now the jets and military spending. Always you will find a reason that you cannot give us aid.[7]

The general discrediting of those who had argued that American aid would solve most of Peru's problems helped to switch the ideological initiative towards those who had argued that loss of political independence was too high a price to pay for the somewhat dubious benefits that the US Treasury provided (or, more often, found excuses not to provide).

This change of emphasis gave an opportunity to various spokesmen from the far-Right, for whom American sponsorship of APRA and social reform was extremely unwelcome, to attack the American government, and in doing so to prove their nationalism and possibly ingratiate themselves with the army.

---

[5] See J. Marichetti and A. Marks, *The C.I.A. and the Cult of Intelligence* (Knopf, New York, 1974), pp. 124–5.

[6] See Villanueva, *El CAEM* . . .

[7] J. Levingston and J. de Onis, *The Alliance that Lost its Way* (Chicago, 1970), p. 138.

The Left also took up the issue, and thus forced the government to comply in public with a condemnation of the American government, whatever further difficulties this might create for its basically pro-American strategy. The cancellation of aid was unanimously condemned in the Chamber of Deputies in early 1968.

Of all the specific irritants in Peruvian–American relations, however, that of the IPC was the longest-standing and was to prove the most decisive. The full history of the IPC conflict cannot be discussed here,[8] but some outline is necessary in order to explain its effect upon military attitudes and upon the decision to intervene. The conflict was important, not only at a legal level, but also because of the values which it revealed and because of its overall position in Peruvian politics.

The International Petroleum Company: The Legal Position

Although legal arguments played a large part in the IPC controversy, there is no general agreement even among lawyers as to the company's true legal position. The main areas of disagreement, however, can be located easily enough. First, there was the question of whether IPC owned the subsoil under its oilfield of *La Brea y Pariñas*. The company claimed a position unique in Peruvian law, which stipulated that only concessions (but not outright subsoil ownership) could be awarded by the state. It appeared that the government had 'illegally' given outright ownership of the deposit to a Peruvian citizen in the 1820s, and that this decision had been ambiguously confirmed by a Peruvian judge in the 1880s. Secondly, there was

---

[8] A full bibliography would be prohibitively long (although Lewis provides a very useful one) but the best general accounts in English are provided by R. Goodwin, op. cit.; S. Lewis, 'The IPC and Peru; a case study of nationalism, management and international relations' (mimeo, California State College at Hayward, 1972); A. Pinelo, *The Multinational Corporation as a Force in Latin American Politics; a case study of the International Petroleum Company in Peru* (New York, 1973), and G. Treverton, 'Politics and Petroleum; the IPC in Peru' (B.A. thesis, Princeton, 1969). In Spanish, there is A. Zimmermann Zavala, *Historia Secreta del Petróleo* (Lima, 1968), and E. Ramirez Novoa, *Recuperación de La Brea y Parinas* (Lima, 1964), and *Petroleo y Revolución Nacionalista* (Lima, 1970). Moreover, for the 1920s there is I. G. Bertram, 'Development Problems of an Export Economy; a study of domestic capitalists, foreign firms and government in Peru 1919–30' (D.Phil., Oxon, 1974), whereas Goodsell, op. cit. (pp. 141–6), is interesting on the 1950s.

dispute over the legal validity of the *Laudo*—an internationally-approved agreement made between IPC and the Peruvian government in 1922, over the exploitation, by IPC, of the *La Brea* field on terms which were extremely disadvantageous for Peru. Thirdly, and crucially, if it were true that the *Laudo* had no validity, there remained the most important question of all —what should be done about it? Answers varied from the conservative view that Peru could not unilaterally repudiate an agreement that had been accepted for so long, and that the most that could be done was to renegotiate the terms with IPC, to the radical view that Peru was entitled to reclaim the entire value of the profits from the *La Brea* oilfield since 1922. The value of this 'debt' would far exceed the value of IPC's total investment in Peru, and extraction of it would entail taking over all of IPC's assets without compensation.

Whatever the arguments of legal scholars, however, it had long been the established view of most politically active Peruvians (including the Peruvian army) that the *Laudo* had not been properly drawn up, and that it was therefore without force. This view was strengthened when, in 1957, IPC's manager applied to the government to transfer from its existing legal status to a concession under the 1952 law. The request was refused but two years later Prime Minister Beltrán did agree to such a transfer. His proposals on this matter led to a major debate within the Peruvian Congress, which culminated in February 1960, when nationalist civilians persuaded the army to declare that they regarded the *Laudo* as null. No political group dared to contradict this view, and Beltrán responded by setting up a commission to look into the problem. This reported that the *Laudo* was illegal, but could not be repudiated unilaterally; according to the commission, the Peruvian government should open negotiations with IPC to try to establish a mutually acceptable legal regime under which it could continue to operate.

After Belaúnde was elected in 1963, Congress found it convenient to take a vaguely nationalist position on the issue. In that year the *Laudo* together with the law of 1918 which had enabled the then-President to take the case to arbitration were formally annulled by Congress. It was more or less understood by the Congressional majority that a negotiated settlement would replace this old legal status. In 1967, with the case still unresolved, Congress repealed another set of decrees, this time dating back to the 1880s. During all this time, IPC and the American government continued to defend the old legal status, at least as a bargaining position, against the almost unanimous view of Peruvians that the *Laudo* was invalid. Meanwhile, the question of what exactly should be done about IPC's unsatisfactory legal position was the issue that divided Peruvians.

These legal differences, however, disguised a far more fundamental conflict. It is unlikely that the admittedly-controversial legal and historical issues would have taken on such significance had there been agreement within Peru on the general principles according to which foreign investment should be treated, and had there been a government capable of putting these into practice. For a long time, however, there was neither ideological conformity nor effective government. Indeed ideological debate over the issue is extremely interesting. It was conducted both within the military and the rest of society and concerned the relative importance of sovereignty and a particular kind of economic avantage. This clash, in turn, partly reflected, and partly helped to define, the conflicting outlooks of military and civilian political elites in the mid-1960s.

The IPC and Political Values

(A) NEOLIBERAL

On one side of the dispute were those—they may be described as 'neoliberals'—who implicitly or openly defended the company. For them, IPC's legal difficulties were less important than the value of its alleged economic contribution to the country. Peru needed private enterprise, it was argued, because the alternative, state control, was inefficient. Thus, *La Prensa* (which was edited by former Prime Minister Beltrán) in typical vein, once described EPF (the small state-owned oil company) as,

a company which runs massive deficits, a refuge for the friends of the government of the day, a deadweight on plans to increase petroleum production, and, in short, a heavy burden for the taxpayer ... and, in general [made up of] incompetents who vegetate at the expense of the sweat of twelve million Peruvians.[9]

[9] *La Prensa*, 31 December 1967.

It went on,

> These *inherent* defects are natural to state enterprise—patronage, wastefulness, lack of economic direction, bureaucratisation, and so forth. (Emphasis mine.)

Similarly, a pro-IPC pressure group, the Peruvian Association of Oilmen, said at a press conference on June 1965,

> We do not consider it necessary to insist on the truism that state administration is generally inefficient.[10]

Indeed, in this view, state enterprise did great harm, not only as a result of its inefficiency, but because it diverted resources from other areas in which they were much needed. As the same Oilmen's Association put it earlier,

> [EPF's money] would have been more wisely invested by the state in roads, schools, hospitals and housing which the country so urgently needed.[11]

The 'neoliberals' were not necessarily opposed to renegotiating with IPC, but were very much against confronting it. Political pressures tended to harden their line towards IPC as the 1960s wore on, but only tactical reasons prevented them from advocating settlement with it on the best terms available. Since they saw no economically satisfactory alternative to continuing to allow IPC to operate, they regarded the controversy as futile and, even worse, bad for business. By turning IPC into a political issue irresponsible people were doing damage to investment and, therefore, national prosperity. The consequence of this was the failure of the Peruvian oil industry. Thus *La Prensa*, after pointing out that it was necessary to increase oil output, added

> and, in order to achieve this objective, we need to abandon completely these demagogic nationalistic posturings which have led us into a situation where we are now importers of petroleum after having been pioneers in its production.[12]

Sometimes the tone turned ugly; thus, a *La Prensa* editorial once declared that IPC's opponents

---

[10] Reported in the *Peruvian Times*, 18 June 1965.
[11] *Peruvian Times*, 18 June 1965.
[12] *La Prensa*, 24 December 1967.

are sabotaging the country as can be seen from those Deputies who have converted the entirely technical problems of petroleum into a truculent history of 'nationalism' and Machiavellian intrigues.[13] From here, it was not very far to supporting repressive measures against the nationalists.

Much emphasis was also placed on the need to attract foreign capital and aid outside the oil industry itself. The IPC case was essentially seen as an irritant to good relations with foreign investors and the American government, with the more traditional conservatives attaching great importance to the former, and the more 'modern' technocrats also showing concern for the latter. Belaúnde's government, in particular, relied very heavily on the support of the United States for massive public expenditure campaigns unbacked by any increase in taxation. Consequently Hoyos Osores (once Belaúnde's Minister of Justice) declared later,

To me, IPC did not matter a fig . . . [what is important] is the foreign investment that the country needs in order to develop.[14]

Belaúnde, in 1964, showed that he felt the same way, by declaring to Congress that he wanted,

a formula by which these [La Brea] deposits will be operated under contract, so resolving the present issue, reaffirming the personality of Peru, assuring greater production, an age of wellbeing and the inflow of international finance in quantities hitherto undreamt of.[15]

These arguments were not contrived *ad hoc*. On the contrary, they were widely used and politically powerful because they echoed the dominant Peruvian political and economic orthodoxy of the period. Petroleum was just another industry, subject to the laws of orthodox economics, and so working best in private—even if foreign—hands. Even for those who were not dogmatically in favour of private investment in all circumstances, taking over IPC would upset foreign financing and might cause problems in the petroleum industry itself. To the *técnicos*, the growth rate was far more important than settling old (and dubious) scores. To the old guard conservatives, IPC

---
[13] 2 July 1967.
[14] In an interview with *Caretas*, 10 December 1969.
[15] Quoted in *El Comercio*, 29 July 1964.

was private property, and that was that. Since it was clear to them that opposition to IPC was damaging the economy, those behind it were clearly subversive demagogues who must be prevented from wreaking havoc in Peru, even if they had to be repressed in the process. Further, quite apart from the fate of the company itself, caving in to radical demands over IPC might only encourage attacks on other American, and even Peruvian, property owners.

This point of view very much reflects the terms under which one side conducted political debate during the 1960s. The economic-liberal orthodoxy was fairly generally held. For the civilian Right, it was fundamental in the absence of any widely acceptable conception of history or authority. As Bourricaud noted

Sr. Beltrán [the Editor of *La Prensa*] is not an intellectual, and does not waste time dreaming of the colonial and pre-Colombian era; he is no more moved by memories of Cuzco than of La Perricholi. He thinks in matter of fact terms; the balance of payments, a sound budget, foreign investment, and the defence of the currency.[16]

Among the 'technocratic reformers' (generally to be found on the right wing of *Acción Popular*), this view was not challenged. These were not so dogmatic about the merits of foreign investment in principle, but relied just as heavily on foreign finance in practice, since their reforms were ambitious, and yet did not involve disturbing those who had economic power. Technical solutions were intended, by definition, to be those which avoided social conflict and these ruled out a hard-line on IPC. Thus, when the Peruvian Association of Oilmen wanted an argument for settlement with the company, they urged that,

it is indispensable that the petroleum problem be dealt with on a technical and economic basis, leaving aside considerations of any other nature.[17]

Not surprisingly, the election of a reformist government after 1963 did not mark a major change in Peru's treatment of IPC, or, indeed, of any other foreign company. As Shane Hunt remarked,

[16] Bourricaud, *Power and Society* . . . , p. 194.
[17] Quoted in the *Peruvian Times*, 18 June 1965.

PERUVIAN NATIONALISM

Despite occasional statements of impatience over economic relations with the United States, and despite somewhat greater severity of terms for foreign investors in petroleum and mining, Peru's favourable view of foreign investment remained unaltered.[18]

This economic liberalism was strengthened, especially after the Cuban revolution, by a tendency towards 'anti-Communism' of the most fundamentalist kind. This was used as a weapon not only against reform of most kinds but also against economic nationalism. In 1960, when Prime Minister Beltrán's proposal to convert IPC into a concessionaire came under attack, the government countered by trying to persuade key army officers that the opponents of the company were dangerous subversives.[19] Later in that year the government launched a concerted campaign to show that these and other opponents were Communists in the pay of Castro. In order to do this, the government appears to have collaborated with the CIA in a raid on the Cuban Embassy. According to Agee,

> The operation was a [CIA] commando raid by Cuban exiles against the Cuban Embassy in Lima which included the capture of documents. The Lima station inserted among the authentic documents several that had been forged by TSD including a supposed list of persons in Peru who received payments from the Cuban Embassy totalling about 15,000 dollars monthly.
> ... Because not may Peruvians believed the documents to be genuine, the Lima station had great difficulty in getting them published. However, a few days ago, a Conservative deputy in the Peruvian Congress presented them for the record, and yesterday they finally surfaced in the Lima press. Although the Cubans have protested that the documents are apocryphal, a recent defector from the Cuban embassy in Lima present during the raid now working for the Agency had 'confirmed' that the TSD documents are genuine. The conservative Peruvian government then used the documents as the pretext for breaking relations with Cuba.[20]

The credibility of these documents was not helped when it was pointed out that one of those named as having received pay from the Cuban embassy had in fact died some time before the Revolution. Nevertheless, the documents provided the excuse

---

[18] S. Hunt in Lowenthal ed., op. cit., p. 306.
[19] See A. Zimmermann, *Historia Secreta*...
[20] P. Agee, *Inside the Company; C.I.A. Diary* (Penguin, London, 1975), p. 146.

which the government needed to gaol some of its opponents and harass most of the rest.

After the 1963 elections, APRA and UNO, who lost the fight for the Presidency, but still had between them a Congressional majority, effectively coalesced around anti-Communist slogans.[21] Periodic charges were then made that Belaúnde's government was Communist infiltrated, and a Congressional committee was set up to investigate charges of Communism among government officials. If Belaúnde had tried any radical measures to settle the IPC case, it is easy to see how the opposition would have countered.

Thus, the Peruvian defenders of IPC were able to excuse what were generally accepted to be legal weaknesses by appealing to a dominant value system that had important and effective application in other areas of society. Although dominant, however, these attitudes were not uniformly held. If they had been, the IPC issue would never have arisen at all. The conflicting sets of values which were drawn upon by the more influential of IPC's opponents were also deeply rooted in Peruvian history, and amounted to a kind of radical nationalism. In fact, the IPC case did much to strengthen these values, and provide a set of supporters for the policies that were pursued by the military government after 1968.

(B) NATIONALIST

The 'nationalist' view, unlike its rival, was not primarily a theory of economics. The core of this view, and the distinguishing mark of its adherents, was the legal demand for the '*revindicación*' of *La Brea*, that is to say, the full recovery of the debt, and the confiscation of IPC in part payment of it. The demand was based on principle, even if it was economically costly in the short run (although it was not necessarily accepted that it would be). Thus, according to Ramirez Novoa,

[21] Indeed, even during the 1962 elections, the candidates campaigned by accusing each other of being soft on Communism. Haya accused Belaúnde thus (see *New York Times*, 4 June 1962) and Odría claimed that 'APRA leaders were Communists in disguise'. (*New York Times*, 10 June 1962). As for the later period, McCoy, op. cit., says that 'Haya de la Torre chose to claim that the Apristas turned to the UNO rather than the Acción Popular because the former shared APRA's firm anti-Communism while Belaúnde's forces were Communist infiltrated. Spokesmen from UNO also justified what was a pragmatic political decision in anti-Communist or ideological terms', p. 350.

The issue of national sovereignty, of defence and security, and of national dignity, is set above everything by the Peruvian people. And only the immediate recuperation of La Brea can bring back tranquillity and confidence to the Peruvian people... we must make it absolutely clear that under no circumstances can we surrender our rich reserves of La Brea for a mess of pottage, because national sovereignty, the dignity of the country, and its economic interests are above any mercenary transaction.[22]

Admittedly, many of IPC's opponents were less intransigent in practice than in theory, but the binding principle of the group was one of 'no compromise' on what was regarded as an essential national interest. As Zimmermann put it,

The problem of *La Brea* was never a purely monetary question for the country. It began as an issue of sovereignty; it later became a set of legal precepts and principles; then it turned into a wistful hope, and it finally emerged as the subject of a major political debate.[23]

For this group, defence of the nation was the fundamental part of the argument. The nationalists were also broadly in favour of public enterprise, since this alone would free Peru from the power and corrupt behaviour of such companies as IPC. Since EPF (which was IPC's only rival) was difficult to defend in its pre-1968 state, the nationalists preferred to attack the neo-liberals for putting obstacles in the path to its development. This was a part of their alleged campaign to defend IPC by frustrating its potential competitor and eventual successor. Thus, according to *El Comercio*,

the campaign, indeed, the whole series of campaigns, that have been carried out against EPF, are well known; depriving it of capital and profits, denying it crude oil for its refinery, and creating obstacles to the marketing of its products; in other words, in order to create an impression that this healthy and able organisation cannot move, it has been tied by the hands and feet.[24]

[22] Ramirez Novoa, *Recuperación*..., pp. 167–71.
[23] *El Comercio*, 4 August 1968.
[24] 16 November 1967. There were also good tactical reasons for defending EPF, since this had been set up by the military (in 1938) and strengthened by successive military governments (in 1952 and 1963). There was, therefore, reason to believe that the military as a whole might take a proprietary interest in the welfare of this company.

The supporters of IPC were also attacked for giving the state a reputation for weakness, which was damaging to overall economic management.

There is a certain blame to be attached to the state, which—by failing to find a solution to the problem of La Brea—has created a climate in which companies are encouraged to be disobedient.[25]

Consequently, IPC had misbehaved,

Peru is faced, as a result of action undertaken by private companies, with the need to import crude oil in order to meet the needs of the internal market ... [there is production potential but] ... making the excuse that 'there are no incentives' for investment, some foreign companies, as in the case of La Brea, have cut back on production. For this reason, because of a policy where the state is not in control but depends on the decision of a foreign monopoly, our country must set aside growing sums of money every year to buy oil abroad when it should be produced at home.[26]

Where incentives did not exist, expropriation might work better.

IPC's opponents were on their most difficult ground over the issue of foreign aid and investment. Their task became easier, however, after the USA had become discredited in Peru by its frequent cancellation of aid. In any case, the credibility of the American threat to cut off aid, if IPC was taken over, was less than total; it was widely suggested that this would not happen. Thus, when Robert Kennedy visited Lima in 1965, he was widely quoted as saying that the Hickenlooper Amendment would not be invoked over IPC—although later an official denial was issued.

This kind of argument had been heard before in Peruvian politics, but it had been very much muted when APRA was identified as the nationalist party. However, the opposition to IPC in the early part of the century, and the resistance to other foreign investors which took place even earlier (whatever the interests that may have been involved), were based on rhetoric of a very similar kind. It was 'radical' in terms of the enemies identified, and in terms of the economic management proposed. It was radical above all in its attitude to civilian political control. The weakness of the government, its 'corruption', its

[25] A. Zimmermann in *El Comercio*, 16 July 1967.
[26] Zimmermann, ibid.

inability to carry out the law in the face of defiance of the nation by a foreign petroleum company, all suggested that the desired solution might lie in a truly national, that is a military, government.

Thus, civilian nationalists made a determined effort to win the army over to their side. Important contacts already existed —*El Comercio* was known to be close to the thinking of a number of army officers, including those who launched the 1968 coup. Indeed, according to one source,

> much of the plotting during the summer and autumn of 1968 went on in an apartment belonging to Alejandro Miró Quesada.[27]

El Comercio could not be regarded as being on the Left. It was, however, fervently anti-Aprista, nationalist on IPC and generally in favour of planning and state enterprise. It backed the coup of 1962, and supported Belaúnde in 1963, but became increasingly unhappy with his soft-pedalling of the IPC issue, and later with his alliance with APRA. These attitudes undoubtedly connected it closely with much military opinion.

A second important civilian group was the *Movimiento Social Progresista* (MSP) led by Alberto Ruíz Eldredge. After its electoral failure in 1962 (when Ruíz Eldredge achieved the remarkable performance of coming bottom of the nine-man poll) the MSP increasingly turned its attentions to the military. The objectives of the party were not very different from those of the Christian Democrats or the left-wing of *Acción Popular*, but its leader took a particularly hard-line on IPC. As Pinelo recounted,

> The opportunity to mingle with the military came when MSP's leader, Alberto Ruíz Eldredge, was invited to speak to the students and staff of the Center for Higher Military Studies (Caem). Ruíz Eldredge used this opportunity to the fullest. He developed close relationships with several Caem officers—much to the annoyance of the I.P.C. management, which had for years sponsored an annual four hour review of the Peruvian petroleum industry at the Center ... Eventually, an officer friendly to I.P.C. attempted to alert the Armed Forces Command to the close relationship between Social Progressist activists and Caem officers, only to be told that the Caem curriculum called for the officers to be exposed to all types of

[27] *Latin America*, 10 August 1973.

philosphical orientations, including Marxism. By the middle 1960's, even though IPC continued to send lecturers to the Center, the officers began to react more and more belligerently towards the company's general manager and his staff, thus indicating that to a very large extent, the Social Progressists were able to persuade Caem officers that their position was valid.[28]

As well as working quietly, however, IPC's opponents occasionally called openly for military intervention on the issue of *La Brea*. In 1959, the civilian nationalists' attack on Beltrán, which was led by Benavides Correa, was clearly aimed at getting a response from within the army. Indeed, only by doing so could they hope to overcome the government majority in Congress. This pattern came to be repeated during the course of Belaúnde's government. Even in 1965, when Belaúnde was still popular, the Odríista, but nationalist, Senator Noriega Calmet asked the military for a statement of its position on IPC.[29] In 1967, the left-wing Populista deputy Villarán made the same request.[30] Later, after the signing of the Act of Talara in August 1968, calls for military intervention came freely from a number of nationalists.

IPC and the Military Coup

The picture emerges, then, of a 'nationalist' lobby which held to a fairly traditional set of values but which was gaining in strength and confidence throughout the 1960s. This was partly because successive governments had found it impossible to settle the dispute while each time an unsuccessful attempt at settlement was made IPC came to be discredited still further.[31] The more general changes in Peruvian politics, however, and the worsening of Peruvian–American relations (as described above) also need to be considered. Under these circumstances, it is not surprising that the support within the army for a radical-nationalist military government was, by 1968, considerable. However, even this is not the whole story. IPC provided

[28] Pinelo, op. cit., p. 95.
[29] *Peruvian Times*, 12 March 1965.
[30] *Latin America*, 4 August 1967.
[31] A more detailed discussion of these attempts during the 1959–68 period appears in the first chapter of G. Philip, 'Policymaking in the Peruvian Oil Industry, with special reference to the period 1968–73' (D.Phil., Oxford, 1975).

not only a radicalizing influence in the long run, but also a golden tactical opportunity in October 1968.

By the middle of that year Belaúnde had at last acquired a Congressional majority. In fact, in June he was given a sixty-day emergency period, during which he would decree legislation without the need for Congressional approval. This period was used for many things, some of which, like the imposition of tax increases, were themselves unpopular. The crucial development, however, was Belaúnde's final attempt to come to an agreement with IPC. By July 1968, the company had also decided that it needed an agreement.[32] It approached Belaúnde and offered to cede the disputed *La Brea* oilfield to the government in return for certain concessions. The government, delighted, re-entered negotiations. These were complex, but the government was in a hurry to have them completed before the 60-day period of emergency powers lapsed and Congressional approval once more became necessary for a settlement. The government's enthusiasm was not matched, however, by another party to the negotiations—Loret de Mola, the head of the state oil company EPF. Although Loret was not opposed on principle to the expected settlement, he was concerned about some of the details and he put up tough resistance to certain of IPC's proposals.

Nevertheless, by 13 August, agreement appeared to have been reached. The Act of Talara was formally signed and it did appear for a time that Belaúnde had a chance of success. Belaúnde's Congressional opponents, as expected, were quick to attack the settlement but, more importantly, *El Comercio* at first refrained from attacking the agreement, and Loret's opposition was not immediately apparent.[33]

Within a month, however, the Act of Talara, and with it Belaúnde's government, had become fatally discredited. His

[32] The reasons for this are explained in Pinelo, op. cit., chapter 6. Basically, IPC had come to feel that its position in La Brea was hopeless, and the company preferred to strike a bargain with a 'friendly' government rather than wait for a confrontation.

[33] The best day-to-day account of the August–October period is provided by Goodwin, op. cit., and see also the account by Zimmermann, *El Plan Inca* . . . , p. 70, although this book should be treated with care, since its author (then Editor of *El Comercio*) needed to explain away his apparent initial acceptance of the Act of Talara and his subsequent change of attitude. There is also chapter 9 of Kuczynski, op. cit., which is written from a pro-Belaúnde standpoint.

serious problems began when several of the Act's less favourable provisions, which had been kept secret at first, gradually leaked out to the press during August—arousing the hostility of *El Comercio* (which may have had information on military attitudes). The decisive blow, however, was felt on 6 September, when the board of EPF (which included General Maldonado Yanez as the army representative) resigned at a time when military opposition to the Act of Talara was already beginning to mobilize. Whatever the reason for this,[34] it was devastating. It was compounded on 10 September when Loret de Mola, appearing on television to give his reasons for resigning, claimed to have discovered that the last page of the contract with IPC had been removed and had disappeared. His public denunciation of this caused many of Belaúnde's supporters (including APRA) to back away from their previous support for the Act of Talara. Belaúnde himself vainly denied Loret's story, tried to stand his ground, but fell victim to a military coup of 3rd October. In the next few days it quickly became clear that the military was prepared to take decisive action against IPC.

Military Attitudes

As we have already seen, it was only in the late 1960s that military opinion hardened decisively against the company. Previously, there had been divisions within the military over the issue, as much as there were everywhere else. Moreover, IPC was only one of the questions with which the military was concerned—and it was often subordinated to the need to support, or desire to oppose, a particular President or political tendency. Thus, in 1931, military President Sánchez Cerro made nationalistic noises over IPC but allowed himself to be bought off by the company.[35] In the mid-1940s, the military opposed Bustamante's attempts to give IPC a concession to explore the Secbura desert, although General Odría's 1952 law allowed them to do so on even more liberal terms.

The next major appearance of the military came in 1960, when it blocked Beltrán's proposals to permit IPC to convert

---

[34] Loret's motives were controversial. Was he in the coup plot, or were his protestations genuine? The latter is more likely if one accepts the considerable circumstantial evidence that p. 11 really was missing. See Goodwin, ibid.

[35] See Pinelo, op. cit., chapter 2.

all of its property to the status of concessionaire under the 1952 petroleum law. As we have seen, this veto may be (at least partly) explained in terms of a general hostility felt towards Beltrán by certain officers. The 1962–3 military government did not take any kind of stand on the IPC question, despite the fact that certain Generals appear to have been pressing for a confrontation on the issue.

IPC was not forgotten, however, when Belaúnde came to power. Thus, according to *Caretas*,

In 1964 the Army set up a military commission, made up of lieutenant colonels, in order to study the problem of La Brea. The President was Col. Morales Bermúdez, now Minister of Finance.

We have found out that this study came to two main conclusions.

1. The state should take charge of the exploitation of the reserves, and should reject any deal with IPC.

2. EPF is technically capable of taking charge of the exploitation of these deposits.[36]

Moreover, according to *Oiga*,[37] in 1965 Caem drew up a plan for the taking of Talara, which provided the basis for the eventual military action. It should be noted, however, that these positions were not necessarily radical—there was no apparent mention of the debt and nothing that excluded the possibility of amicable settlement with IPC. In fact, the Act of Talara apparently met the criteria laid down by the army in 1964.

Evidence of military attitudes to the issue in 1968 is incomplete and often ambiguous, but it is certain that military doubts and internal differences remained until a very late stage. There can be no doubt that IPC was widely regarded with intense suspicion and dislike,[38] but it was not always clear on what terms, if any, the military would accept settlement of the dispute. IPC itself was not terribly worried about the military; its

[36] *Caretas*, 16 April 1968.
[37] *Oiga*, 8 November 1968.
[38] Goodwin, op. cit., tells the story that, after the devaluation of 1967, IPC asked for a compensating price rise, and was refused. The company then threatened to stop production. The General Manager of IPC was then summoned to the Presidential Palace and roundly told off by the Army Chief of Staff Gen. Doíg. He then asked permission to return to headquarters to ring IPC's head office in Florida, but was told to stay and use the telephone in the building.

General Manager, Fernando Espinoza... had held personal meetings with Gens. Julio Doíg Sánchez and Fransisco Morales Bermúdez [who were rumoured to be plotting a coup] and found them well-disposed towards the company.[39]

Despite everything, therefore, the attitude of the military hardened only after the Act of Talara and the subsequent scandal over the disappearance of p. 11. Even after the coup had taken place, however, the military was still divided on the issue of the final *revindicación* of La Brea. It is almost certain that Velasco was already interested in launching a coup for reasons that had nothing to do with the question of IPC and that much of the army was not greatly moved by it (either supporting the coup on other grounds or opposing it altogether), but it seems that the Act of Talara was a 'swing issue' that enabled Velasco to get enough support to make a success of the coup which he was already planning. According to Goodwin,[40] thirty-six generals held a secret meeting in September to discuss the Act of Talara. Velasco later described the outcome as being 'twenty nine against the agreement, and seven traitors'. From these twenty-nine were drawn the leaders of the coup.

Conclusions

The nationalism of the Peruvian military can be attributed to changes which took place at a variety of levels. In an ideological sense, opposition to IPC was based on a semi-traditional concern for national sovereignty, which was a rival to the alternative belief system based on *laissez-faire* liberalism, and firm anti-Communism. For a long time this nationalism had been effectively suppressed by an overriding concern to prevent Aprista, and later 'Communist', social revolution. As was the case in Brazil during the early 1950s, the military in the last resort was more concerned with order than national sovereignty. The course of Peruvian politics during the 1950s and 1960s had acted to undermine this fear, however, and consequently it appeared that a programme of nationalist reform could be led by the military itself. Moreover, the change in the intellectual climate which took place during the 1960s greatly increased the

[39] Pinelo, op. cit., p. 137.
[40] Goodwin, op. cit., p. 88.

importance placed upon national autonomy in the course of economic development and provided another powerful argument for state control. What had long been politically desirable, now became economically respectable.

This change in military attitudes was catalysed by a number of specific disputes between the Peruvian military and the American government, which built up a catalogue of resentments which were to be expressed under the Velasco regime. The American government's decision to intervene more directly in Latin American politics after the Cuban revolution led in Peru to a nationalist reaction on the part of an institution which had previously earned a justified reputation for being conservative and pro-American. This reaction can be attributed initially to American support for APRA in the 1962 elections, which was followed by a refusal to recognize the Peruvian military government after the coup, and subsequently to American intervention in what the military regarded as its own sphere of action. This took place first in 1965 when the U.S. government intervened directly to counter the guerrilla movement, bypassing much of the regular Peruvian army, and later in 1967–8 when American refusal to sell supersonic planes to Peru was followed by a cutoff of aid after the Peruvian government purchase of Mirages.

Finally, the messiness of Belaúnde's attempted solution of the IPC dispute provided an almost perfect excuse for direct military intervention. The saga of leaked terms, missing pages, and charges of betrayal, completely destroyed the credibility of the government, and the coup of 3rd October surprised nobody except Belaúnde himself. Those army officers who were already plotting intervention had good reason for gratitude towards those responsible for the Act of Talara.

III

THE MILITARY GOVERNMENT 1968-69 COMPOSITION AND OUTLOOK

Any military *coup d'état* involves a wide range of officers and therefore a variety of motivations. One of the few case studies which has been made of a Latin American coup stressed the fact that,

investigation revealed that ... groups and cliques clustered around particular individuals, of quite diverse political orientation and motives.[1]

Within limits the same was true of the Peruvian military coup of 1968. This is not to say that overall political considerations were unimportant, but rather that the coup and its immediate aftermath brought together a set of military officers who could not possibly have acted together over a longer term. Thus, between the moment of the coup and the final emergence of a stable military government a period of political definition, and therefore of political conflict, was inevitable.

Within the Peruvian military government of October 1968 there were those who intended only minor changes, and who had been reluctant to support the coup at all. There were others, however, who saw the seizure of government as merely a prelude to a complete overhaul of Peruvian politics and society, such as to ensure that there could be no return to the pattern of politics that had existed prior to 1968. The conflict between these two tendencies was fought out in the early months of the military government, and resulted in victory for the radicals. This outcome and its consequences cannot be understood without reference to the broader political and ideological issues in Peru, which have already been discussed. At the same time, however, the conflict itself, and the manner in which it was resolved, are themselves important to the understanding of the emergent military government.

[1] M. Needler's study of the 1963 coup in Ecuador, quoted in J. Miguens, 'The New Latin American Military Coup', in *Studies in Comparative International Development* (1970–1, pp. 3–12), p. 6.

Coup Leaders

(A) GENERAL VELASCO

General Juan Velasco Alvarado appears to have been a disillusioned former supporter of Belaúnde. He had undoubtedly been planning a coup for some time before he finally moved in October 1968: he himself estimated that the waiting period lasted a full year.[2] In any case, the events of 1968—which had seen Belaúnde reject Velasco's proposal that he dissolve Congress, and govern with military support, and then pass Velasco over as Minister of War in mid-1968—crystallized Velasco's determination, while the other events of that year made the coup possible.

No matter how strongly motivated Velasco may have been, however, there was nothing in his background to mark him out as a radical; indeed, his relations with the Prado family went back several years; 'when Manuel [Prado] was still in office, Mariano had intervened on Velasco's behalf to save his career from a hostile minister of war ... Some members of the Prado family had maintained personal ties to Velasco; Max Pena Prado, for instance, had been an usher at his wedding'.[3] Later, Velasco is said to have been deeply impressed by de Gaulle when he acted as military *attaché* in Paris. *Caretas* initially described him as a conservative nationalist.

Velasco's background was lower-middle class and provincial. He was born in Piura in 1909, finished secondary school but joined the army as a private in order to save enough money to buy a uniform and enter the Chorrillos academy. He was the son-in-law of a prominent Aprista, but did not allow any sympathies that he might have felt towards that party to block his career. According to Gall,

Velasco's first important post on the bureaucratic ladder of the army was director of Chorrillos from 1950 to 1953 under the violently anti-Aprista dictatorship of General Manuel Odría. One of Velasco's

---

[2] General Velasco discusses his role in an interview with N. Moreira, *Modelo Peruano* (La Linea, Buenos Aires, 1974). *La Prensa's* Sunday supplement (*Siete Dias*, 6 October 1968) also carried the interesting story that, in the summer of 1968, Belaúnde's War Minister, General Gagliardi, arranged a meeting between Manuel Ulloa (Belaúnde's Finance Minister) and Velasco in order to try to win the support of the latter for the government's austerity measures, but Velasco flatly refused this support.

[3] Gilbert, 'The Oligarchy...', p. 259.

main tasks as head of Chorrillos was to instill in the cadets a fervent fear and hatred of APRA and Velasco had to be especially convincing in this.[4]

From then he rose steadily but unspectacularly and without involving himself too openly in politics.

(B) VELASCO'S COLONELS

Velasco's keenest and most ideologically motivated supporters in the coup were a group of radical Colonels. The influence of this group can be seen in the coup manifesto which was issued the day after the takeover of power,

Powerful economic forces—both national and foreign with Peruvian support—being motivated by overwhelming greed, retain political and economic power and frustrate the popular desire for basic structural reforms ... our resources have been compromised under conditions of notorious disadvantage to the country in such a way as to bring about its dependence upon economic power, affront our sovereignty and indefinitely postpone every change that would make it possible for us to overcome our present condition of underdevelopment.[5]

Although much of their rhetoric is at a high level of abstraction, and so difficult to evaluate, it incorporates many of the ideas put forward by 'dependency' writers who sought to explain Latin America's underdevelopment in terms of its connection, through the world capitalist system, to the economically dominant powers of Europe and the United States. Overall, the objectives of the radical Colonels could best be described as 'revolution from above'. Wide ranging reforms were to be introduced to reduce or eliminate Peru's poverty and social injustice, and, at the same time, to transform the Peruvian economy. These could only be carried out during the course of a long period of military government. During this time, existing political institutions were to be eliminated, and replaced by participatory systems which the military government would plan and introduce.

One strand in the thinking of these military radicals appears to have been a refusal to recognize the legitimacy of social

[4] N. Gall in *Dissent* (1971, pp. 281–320) p. 307.
[5] Quoted in V. Trias, op. cit., p. 118.

conflict, and a desire to impose a kind of authoritarian collectiveism under which such conflict would no longer occur. As one observer pointed out,

> The influence of radical Catholic ideas on the military leaders of Peru cannot perhaps be overstressed. A great deal of the official rhetoric dwells on the need to create a 'new man' (sounds just like Guevara, as one Uruguayan journalist remarked), and a qualitatively different society from which the objective causes of class conflict will have been removed. The military recognise the existence of class struggle in Peru, due to the mechanisms of exploitation and private appropriation of wealth, and they believe it must be overcome, not just by exhorting the rich and powerful to have a change of heart, but by concrete structural changes in the relations between the social classes.[6]

Thus, the oligarchy, which had allegedly governed Peru for so long, was to be destroyed and the influence (and earnings) of foreign companies were to be drastically reduced. Immediately after the takeover of power, the objectives of the radicals were the *revindicación* of IPC, and the carrying out of a comprehensive land reform. Wide ranging reforms were then expected to follow.

Some of the immediate reforms on the agenda were based on plans drawn up at Caem.[7] Nevertheless, the overall objectives of this group were altogether more radical than those taught at Caem, whose direct influence on them was limited. Indeed, five of the most radical Colonels—Fernández Maldonado, Leonidas Rodríguez, Gallegos, Váldez Palacio and Molina— never graduated from the centre.[8] In any case, Caem doctrine was far less radical than the manifesto even if some similarities could be detected. The attitudes of most of this group, in fact, appear to have been formed by experiences of military intelligence and counter-insurgency. Gallegos had helped to carry out a land reform in *La Convención* under the 1962–3 military government, after the activities of Hugo Blanco in the valley

---

[6] C. Harding, 'Peru; Questions of Revolution', pp. 185–90 of the *Latin American Review of Books*, vol. 1, Spring 1973, pp. 188–9.

[7] See *Oiga*, 8 November 1968.

[8] See C. Astiz and J. Garcia, 'The Peruvian Military; Achievements, Orientation, Training and Political Tendencies', in *Western Political Quarterly*, November 1972, p. 675.

had led the government to order military intervention.[9] Moreover, almost all of this group had been active in countering the 1965 guerrilla movement, and this had clearly been a radicalizing experience (although, as we shall see, not all officers were influenced in the same way). At least some of them had military intelligence jobs after 1965, and so were responsible for monitoring peasant attitudes. At a more personal level, they may have developed a certain cohesion from the fact that, as a group, they had graduated from the Escuela Militar de Chorrillos in the early 1940s.

Given the radical intentions of these officers, they may well have been influenced by their contacts with Left-wing civilians.[10] Caem does appear to have taken on some significance in these discussions, but only in as far as it provided a meeting-ground. These conversations, however, do appear to have been quite close; indeed, one observer suggested that,

the transformation of the Peruvian military from a provincial constabulary to an insurgent force challenging U.S. policy in Latin America probably would have been impossible without an increasingly intimate dialogue with leftist intellectuals, such as took place at the Caem between high army officers and the leaders of the mini-parties of Peru's 'little Left' who today [1971] serve as advisers to the 'Revolutionary government'.[11]

(c) GENERAL MONTAGNE

Apart from Velasco himself, however, the most important single figure in the coup was General Ernesto Montagne Sánchez. Indeed, in October 1968, a number of sources saw him as the power behind the throne.[12] However, rather little is known about his motivations at that time, and these therefore must be explored through his past history and later political attitudes. Montagne came from a military family and so inherited family loyalties. He was strongly anti-Odríista because Odría had imprisoned his father for daring to stand for the

[9] See above, p. 39.
[10] Military contacts with the civilian anti-IPC lobby were discussed in the previous chapter.
[11] N. Gall, op. cit., p. 311. Indeed, Left-wing civilians played important parts in drafting the most important reform laws which the regime implemented.
[12] See, for example, *Caretas*, 14 October 1968.

Presidency against him (a move which had been made with the support of the Southern opposition). In fact, he appears to have been a supporter of Belaúnde, under whom he served as Minister of Education for a year. He then played a major role in putting down the 1965 guerrilla movement, and was known to be unhappy about Congressional criticisms of Belaúnde at that time.[13] Politically Montagne took a hard-line on IPC; he made this clear as early as 9th October, when he declared that,

the only company with a constitutional problem in Peru is the IPC. When questions of dignity and national sovereignty are involved, any material sacrifice is always wholly justifiable.[14]

Since Cardinal Landázuri was his brother-in-law, he may also have been influenced by the attitude of the Church, which had publicly denounced the Act of Talara prior to the coup. Montagne was relatively conservative on other issues.

(D) GENERAL MALDONADO

Another figure to have been directly involved in the coup, General Maldonado was a man of very different complexion. He had connections with another active-duty Colonel, Gonzales Briceño, who had been in charge of the operation to arrest Belaúnde on the night of the coup. Relations between these two dated back at least to 1965 when, according to Marichetti's account,

Green Berets participated in what was the CIA's single large-scale Latin American intervention of the post-Bay of Pigs era. In Peru, in 1965.

Unable to cope adequately with the insurgent movement, Lima had turned to the U.S. government for aid, which was immediately and covertly forthcoming... As the training progressed, and the efficiency of the counter-guerrilla troops increased, the Peruvian government grew uneasy...

A few months later, when Peru was celebrating its chief national holiday, the authorities refused to allow the CIA-trained troops into the capital for the annual military parade. Instead, they had to settle for marching through the streets of a dusty provincial town, in a satellite observance of the great day. Realising that many a Latin American regime had been toppled by a crack regiment, Peru's

[13] On which, see the *New York Times*, 1 August 1965.
[14] *Caretas*, 14 October 1968.

leaders were unwilling to let the CIA force even come to Lima and the government soon moved to dismantle the unit.[15]

The Rangers' commander was Colonel Gonzales Briceño, who was subsequently denied both recognition and promotion. As Astiz noted,

It was no accident that Col. Gonzales Briceño, who led the takeover of the Presidential palace in the 1962 coup d'etat, was still a colonel when he led a remarkably similar operation on October 3, 1968.[16]

As military commander of the Cuzco region, Maldonado must have been aware of Gonzales Briceño's connections. Indeed, it is reported that, once the 1965 campaign had ended, he was upset that Belaúnde had given him only a lukewarm congratulation, and pleased that the American Defence Secretary, McNamara, had given him a much warmer one.[17] After his 1965 experiences, Maldonado became a member of the board of the state petroleum company, EPF. The composition of this board was fairly moderate, and it certainly showed no early sign that it would make things difficult for Belaúnde. Nevertheless, its eventual resignation on 6 September, in protest against certain provisions of the Act of Talara, was a severe, possibly decisive blow against the government. During this period, General Maldonado kept a low profile, and is said to have kept in close touch with his army colleagues. In fact, it appears that General Maldonado represented the more conservative sections of the army who were prepared to take a superficially hard-line on IPC in order to justify taking power and blocking Belaúnde's alliance with APRA.

On 3 October, therefore, this relatively small group of officers and their friends took over the government and presented the rest of the military with a *fait accompli*. The generals close to Belaúnde (Gagliardi, Dianderas and Linares, as well as Admiral Sánchez Salazar) were forced out. Several others were

---

[15] Marichetti and Marks, op. cit., pp. 124–5. Even before this, however, Colonel Briceño had been tied in closely with the United States military. Thus, according to a report in 1962, Briceño headed 'a crack anti-guerrilla commando unit which was a showpiece of the U.S. military mission'. (*New York Times*, 21 July 1962). As a result of this, Briceño's participation in the 1962 military coup was a source of some embarrassment to the American government.

[16] C. Astiz, *Pressure Groups* . . ., p. 168.

[17] *Caretas*, 14 October 1968.

in conveniently remote locations at the time; General Rodríguez Razetto was in Washington, General Valdivia was in Arequipa, General Malaga was in the North, General Benavides was in Iquitos, and General Artola was in Piura. The navy and air force were not brought into the coup, although some of their officers later joined the government.

The First Military Government: Composition

After launching the coup, Velasco and Montagne had to bring in many of these other officers in order to create an 'institutional' base for the military government. Thus, in many cases, the actual authors of the coup made way in the Council of Ministers for their more senior and conservative colleagues. It was the conflict between these two groups—the radical coup leaders, and the more conservative senior officers—that was fought out at the beginning of 1969.

One of the more prominent conservative members of the new government was General José Benavides. He was the son of a military President, wealthy, and one of the very few officers to be connected with private companies (notably Cerro de Pasco). He was distantly related to Haya de la Torre, and his father had been relatively close to APRA and to the Prado family (as well as being a close friend of the father of General Montagne). Benavides was very popular with the officer corps and he was also a favourite of *La Prensa* (which devoted a supplement to him on 6 October). He became Minister of Agriculture and, in doing so, convinced a number of observers that the Peruvian government was not serious about agrarian reform.

Another major figure to come into the Council of Ministers was the commander of the Arequipa division, General Valdivia. Valdivia was an intellectual disciple of *La Prensa*, with a strong belief in foreign investment and a balanced budget. He was thus close to a number of Odríistas, and he quickly selected one of the more prominent of these, Sr Berckemeyer, for a top job in his ministry.

General Mercado Jarrín who became Foreign Minister might have been expected to provide more support for the radicals. Mercado was a military intellectual (he had been at the head of a military training centre when the coup took place) and something of a theorist. He appears to have been yet another disappointed former supporter of Belaúnde; according to Niera, Mercado,

said privately in 1967 that the army had lost confidence in Belaúnde because he was gutless and had not achieved the reforms the country had hoped for and needed.[18]

Before the coup, he had spent much of his time trying to relate Caem doctrine to the perceived need for thorough social reform. According to Einaudi,

In a formal intelligence analysis by General Mercado ... the 'latent stage of subversion' was defined as the presence of Communist activity exploiting national weaknesses. This Communist activity, which took a variety of forms, military, political, economic and social, was containable for the present. But the existence of national weaknesses continually threatened to point the balance against the forces of progress and order. National weak spots were defined, in General Mercado's remarkable statement of this theory, to cover a wide range of organisational, economic, technical and political elements ... The reforms introduced by the revolutionary military government that took office less than a year after Mercado's article had appeared were largely meant to offset these weaknesses.[19]

Another army general to join the Council of Ministers was Artola, who was a close personal friend of Velasco. Artola came from a military family (his father had been a Cabinet Minister under Odría) and he had been chief of army intelligence at the time of the guerrilla movement. After the coup, he became Minister of the Interior, and began his new job by removing documents connected with a smuggling scandal, declaring a 'moralization' campaign, and suppressing *Caretas*.[20]

The navy and air force were also brought into the military government, although the air force was given only three portfolios and the navy two. Vice-Admiral Navarro, one of only two naval officers to have had prior knowledge of the coup, was

[18] Niera, op. cit., p. 464.
[19] Einaudi, 'Changing patterns ...', pp. 17–18.
[20] N. Gall, op. cit., p. 309. The suppression of *Caretas* was due to the fact that it, alone of the Peruvian newspapers, made a serious effort to dissect the coup thus breaking an unwritten rule that divisions within the military should not be discussed openly. There was also a personal element in Artola's reactions to *Caretas*, since the latter had embarrassed him at the time of the guerrilla movement by giving the insurgents full and relatively sympathetic coverage.

made Minister of Justice, while Admiral Pardo de Zela, who accepted the coup as a fact, briefly became Navy Minister.[21] The politics of the navy were complicated, and its political strength was weakened, by the fact that many of its members appear to have been involved in a smuggling scandal that broke in early 1968. This scandal was successfully hushed up at the time by threats of military intervention; in any case, it seemed that the Apristas, who came into possession of most of the details, were less interested in the impartial administration of justice than in the blackmailing of their opponents. Nevertheless, the scandal did have longer-run implications. According to one source,

A few days after the coup, army troops surrounded the vacant building of Congress in downtown Lima and removed a large quantity of documents, including a list of high-ranking officers implicated in the contraband scandals. Among those involved were the navy minister, the naval intelligence chief, and the director of the P.I.P. The Navy Minister [Pardo de Zela] and the PIP director were forced to resign, but the naval intelligence chief [Carbonel] survived to head a 'moralisation' purge of the Finance Ministry and the Central Bank.[22]

The air force was also unhappy with the coup, although it did eventually agree to join the government.[23] Nevertheless, Air Force General López Casilles, who took the Aviation Ministry was never in sympathy with the government, or very popular personally among his colleagues. He resigned within a month of the coup. The official reason for his resignation was disagreement about military promotions. In fact, according to *La Prensa*, López resigned because of Velasco's plans to promote officers loyal to himself over the heads of the existing air force leadership.[24] Once he did resign, Velasco did precisely that; passing over Jose Heighes, Jorge Soldi and Rolando Gervasi, who were all friends of each other, promoting Gilardi to Aviation Minister, and bringing Chamot (who was one of only two

---

[21] See *Expreso*, 6 October 1968 and A. Z. Zimmermann, *El Plan Inca; objectivo revolución peruana* (O.N.I., Lima, 1974).

[22] N. Gall, op. cit., p. 309. Baella, in *El Poder Invisible*, suggests that Velasco was himself involved in the scandal, but his evidence does not justify his accusation.

[23] Zimmermann, op. cit.

[24] *La Prensa*, 27 October 1968.

air force officers to have had prior knowledge of the coup) into the Council of Ministers.

However, immediately after the coup, the Council of Ministers was:

Velasco's Allies	Conservatives	Others
Gen. Velasco (President)	Gen. Benavides (Agriculture)	Gen. Montagne (Prime Minister)
Gen. Artola (Min. of Government)	Gen. Maldonado (Development)	Gen. Mercado (Foreign Minister)
Gen. Arrisueño (Min. of Education)	Gen. Valdivia (Finance)	A. F. G. Montero (Health)
A. F. G. Gilardi (Min. of Labour)	A. F. G. López (Aviation)	
	Vice Adm. Navarro (Navy)	

Velasco found places for 'his' Colonels in a newly-founded presidential secretariat (Coap). This included Leonídas Rodríguez, Fernández Maldonado and Meza Cuadra and was headed by Cavero Calixto (who was later replaced by José Graham).[25] All of these became Generals at the beginning of 1969.

Civilian Allies

Civilian political support for the government was as diverse as its own composition. Some came from certain very prominent people of the Right. These included Berckemeyer (who had been a good friend of Odría) and Raul Ferrero (who had taught at Caem) both of whom were linked to the Atlas Security company.[26] These may have been partly motivated by personal rivalry with Ulloa who had financial connections and who was regarded as something of an upstart in older and less efficient enterprises. Also, the influence of the Prado family may have been important. The Ayulo family, which held shares in the Banco de Credito apparently supported the coup in the hope of reducing the influence of the Prados on the incoming military government.[27]

[25] Zimmermann, op. cit., provides a full list of COAP members, p. 144.
[26] *Caretas*, 14 October 1968.
[27] Gilbert, op. cit., pp. 154–5.

The Prados themselves were particularly warm supporters of the military coup. Indeed,

> according to several sources ... [they] ... gave the military a considerable sum of money to help finance [it] ... [later] the Prados were on particularly good terms with the government and had easy access to the President ... In April 1969, when the government was apparently in the midst of an effort to gain investor confidence, Mariano Prado led a group of bankers which publicly declared its support of the regime.[28]

The Prados' main concern was less with overall government policy than their need to secure government consent to their sale of Banco Popular to a subsidiary of the Chase Manhattan.

Apart from these personal contacts, some conservatives supported the coup out of fear that Belaúnde (in possession of a Congressional majority after his alliance with APRA) might start to carry out reforms and, indeed, resentment at the tax increases already imposed in July 1968.[29] The Right had reason to remember previous periods of military rule favourably, when the Apristas had been held at bay and free enterprise encouraged. Even in 1962–3, when there were radical tendencies within the military government, the Right had eventually triumphed. This time, the result might be repeated.

The military also had the support of the anti-IPC lobby. This included some conservatives, perhaps also influenced by the reasons given above, such as the Miró Quesada family (owners of *El Comercio*) and Mario Herrera Gray, who was a prominent Odriista. More radical figures were also prominent in opposition to IPC, and thus supported the military government. These included Ruíz Eldredge, Ramirez Novoa and Benavides Correa. It is not clear how much prior knowledge this group had of the coup, but they clearly made their presence felt soon after. According to *Caretas*,

> according to generally well informed sources, the Manifesto was composed by Mario Herrera Grey, Alfonso Baella and Augusto

---

[28] Ibid., pp. 154–5.
[29] Thus, Leon Velarde, a prominent Right-wing politician, who was head of the *Comando Nacional de las Barriadas*, welcomed the coup on the grounds that taxes were too high (*Latin America*, 10 October 1968). It was perhaps fitting that, after spending a period as Artola's deputy in the Interior Ministry, Velarde was arrested in 1975 on charges of tax evasion (see *Oiga*, 31 October 1975).

Zimmermann ... Participation is also attributed to Alfonso Benavides Correa, who had called for a coup on a TV programme, and Ezequiel Ramirez Novoa, who, it is said, was asked by the military for his opinions on copper.[30]

Finally, as we have seen, much of the civilian Left—finally disillusioned with Belaúnde—had already turned their attentions to the military and were only too eager to strengthen and advise its radical faction.

Evolution of the Government's Political Base; October 1968 to January 1969

It was evident that this coalition was far too wide to support a government. It could not agree on any important action, but neither could it yield gracefully to a successor. Some conflict would have to occur before the direction of policy could be established. Moreover at least one important group had obviously overestimated its political strength, and would quickly be defeated. The issue which produced the first, and most important, internal political confrontation concerned IPC. The initial decision to take over the Talara complex on 9 October was apparently itself controversial.[31] The repudiation of the Act of Talara and the take over of the Talara complex, however, did not necessarily imply the *revindicación* of La Brea. Certainly U.S. business was not seriously worried at this early stage, and regarded the military move as an act of showmanship which would be followed by a fresh set of negotiations. In fact, military intentions were not exactly clear but diplomatic discussion with the U.S.A. and informal contacts with IPC continued for the rest of the year.

It was the issue of total confiscation that seriously divided the government. The hard-line opponents of IPC achieved an initial success in late October, when Ruíz Eldredge, who

[30] *Caretas*, 14 October 1968. Zimmermann, *El Plan Inca* ..., says that the manifesto was last seen by Colonels Cavero Calixto, Leonídas Rodriguez and Fernández Maldonado. Both accounts are likely to be true. Certainly other press accounts suggested that the radical Colonels had played a major part in drawing up the manifesto. See D'Ornellas' article in *Expreso*, 6 October 1968.

[31] An article in the *Financial Times* (8 October 1968) was the first to suggest that the Central Bank opposed this move.

happened to be the senior lawyer on the Lima bar as well as a long-time opponent of IPC, was entrusted with preparing the government's case against the company. The most prominent of the military hardliners was Velasco himself. According to *Caretas*,

> The petroleum crisis, and its symptoms (silence) has not afflicted all members of the Junta in the same way. In fact, Gen. Juan Velasco Alvorado has hardly spoken about anything else in the last few days than petroleum and the threats flying about in consequence.[32]

In fact Velasco's position was decisive in ensuring his survival. In October his political position was far from secure. His retirement date was coming up at the beginning of 1969; many officers would have been pleased to see him go, and a number of observers believed that he would.[33] However, the question of his departure was submitted to a 'sounding' process within the military, and the feeling was that he should stay. This decision had much to do with the hard-line position which Velasco took over IPC, and it is important to examine how.

One major explanation for the hard-line on IPC stems from the position of the military in Peruvian politics. The coup, not surprisingly, had made enemies. The most important of these were the supporters of Belaúnde and the Apristas. Combined together, as they were, they could easily have commanded an electoral majority under existing rules. There was thus no question—as there had been in 1963—of calling elections, allowing the candidate of the military to win, and returning to barracks. Experience of Belaúnde's government, in any case, did not make a repeat performance seem attractive. Many officers, after all, had concluded that Belaúnde's failure was due to the fact that real power in Peru was held by economic interests rather than elected politicians, and they therefore saw no reason to relinquish power before carrying out a comprehensive series of reforms.

[32] *Caretas*, 12 December 1968.
[33] Those who expected his departure included *Caretas*, *Oiga* and *Business Latin America*.
The Chirinos Soto brothers' book *El Septenatio* (Lima, 1977) includes an interesting and detailed account of events surrounding the question of Velasco's survival in late 1968. *El Septenatio* places a lot of emphasis on the support given to Velasco by *El Comercio* (largely as a result of Zimmermann's manoeuverings).

COMPOSITION AND OUTLOOK 89

Thus, the military decided to rule alone, for some time at least. Indeed, even from the very beginning, it was clear that the regime had no immediate intention of calling elections. Since this was so, it was important for the military to win popularity, and perhaps the only way of doing this was to take a hard line on IPC. Moreover, while the takeover of the Talara complex may have done something to increase military popularity, this initial advantage had been dissipated by the end of the year as a result of uncertainty over the future course of the government. A pro-regime demonstration, called on 20 December, proved to be a disappointment, and was greatly surpassed in size by a pro-Aprista demonstration in January 1969. This may have persuaded a number of officers that a nationalist initiative was needed.[34] After all, populist politicians elsewhere in Latin America had followed Castro's example and drawn vast crowds to hear vigorous denunciations of the U.S. government and 'foreign imperialism'. Why couldn't the Peruvian military do the same?

In any case, IPC was an issue on which compromise was impossible. The appointment of Ruíz Eldredge as lawyer for the government virtually ensured that a choice would have to be made on the issue of *revindicación*. Anything less could only be interpreted as a defeat for the nationalists. The political tactics adopted by the Right added to this polarization. From December 1968, two opposition newspapers, *Expreso* (which was pro-Belaúnde) and *La Prensa* (which was more specifically anti-Velasco) attempted to discredit the government by revealing that IPC had sent US $17m. out of the country after October, with the permission of members of the military government. They suggested that Velasco was less of a nationalist than he pretended. Unfortunately for them, however, this tactic backfired. Feeling against IPC intensified, and Velasco's political position was strengthened. It was especially unfortunate for *La Prensa* that General Valdivia, who opposed the policy of confrontation with IPC, was Finance Minister at the time and so directly responsible for the outflow of dollars.

[34] One observer euphemistically pointed out that the pro-government demonstration 'did not have the strength that its promoters hoped for' and that this was a factor in the move towards a more radical position. J. Aguilar Derpich, *Perú; ¿Socialismo Militar?* (Caracas, 1972) p. 89.

Given these considerations, Velasco was able to split his opponents by taking a hard-line stand over the IPC issue. Some key officers, who had been expected to turn against Velasco when the question of his retirement came up, did not in fact do so. Velasco was undoubtedly helped by the fact that he had already been able to overcome opposition from within the air force whose new head—Gilardi—was a firm supporter of Velasco, and by the weakness of the navy, which Velasco had used to promote his friends Navarro and Carbonel. The real factor in his survival, however, was opinion in the army. Here, only Generals Maldonado Yanez and Valdivia opposed him intransigently.

These two were themselves unpopular. They had supported IPC's position in the Council of Ministers, and argued that economic sanctions had to be avoided at all costs. Both of them appear to have had links with the USA. Valdivia was the American government's preference for President, a somewhat dubious distinction,[35] and Maldonado (along with his opponents) may have remembered the events of 1965. Moreover, Valdivia was a fervent believer in fiscal austerity; he was preparing a very severe deflationary budget for 1969, which, according to one source,

set many industrialists and public sector employees against him, contributing to his downfall.[36]

Finally, Valdivia does not appear to have had any kind of personal following within the officer corps.

Indeed, Valdivia's open stand against Velasco may even have worked in the latter's favour, by inhibiting the more formidable opposition that might have been provided by Montagne or Benavides. Neither of these Generals would have been eager to support the Odriista faction of the army, and they may well have preferred to take their chance with Velasco who was still something of an unknown quantity. Both of them shared Velasco's hard-line position on IPC, and neither would

[35] See *Business Latin America*, 16 January 1969, and *Latin America*, 4 April 1969. Janet Ballantine also provides some interesting insights (derived from a contact in the American Embassy) in chapter 2 of 'The Political Economy...'. According to her, the American Embassy persuaded Valdivia of the correctness of IPC's position only to see him removed from office largely in consequence.

[36] *Latin America*, 4 April 1969.

have been happy to follow the alternative programme of fiscal austerity, domestic repression and concessions to American interests. On the other hand, once Valdavia and Maldonado had initiated their attack on Velasco's position, it was no longer possible for Montagne to use the conservative majority that existed in the Council of Ministers to block the more radical of Velasco's initiatives. He was faced instead with a very difficult choice.

In fact, Montagne's failure to press home his early opposition to Velasco was a key factor in the latter's survival. While there is no hard evidence, it is likely that certain personal as well as political factors were important in his decision. His dislike of Odría and his supporters has already been noted. Moreover, given the fact that his brother-in-law was Cardinal Archbishop of Lima, Montagne must have been influenced by the attitude of the Church, which was outspokenly in favour of military reformism. Finally, personality undoubtedly played a part. Montagne has never given the impression of being a particularly strong or dynamic figure; he seems to have had rather little influence over the Velasco government even when he was its Prime Minister. Whatever the reason, Montagne held back and Velasco survived.

Consolidation; early 1969

Once Velasco's power was assured, he moved decisively against his opponents on all fronts. He needed to reward his own supporters, and reduce the political diversity of the government to manageable levels. The major confrontation with IPC, therefore, occurred in late January and early February 1969, culminating on 6 February with the announcement of IPC's US $690m. debt to Peru. At the same time, certain governmental changes occurred. These took place after the Council of Ministers announced the setting up of a commission, headed by Admiral Carbonel and including a number of radical civilians (including the ever-present Ruíz Eldredge) to investigate the disappearance of the US $17m. from IPC's bank account.

The objective of the commission was clearly political—to provide the basis for a purge of those whose loyalty to the government was suspect. It seems that Admiral Carbonel could be controlled by the government because of his involvement in the smuggling scandal. In any case, the formation of the commission led to the resignation of Generals Valdivia and Maldonado from the Council of Ministers. When the commission reported, there followed a purge of the Central bank and the removal of the head of EPF. There were political grounds for both of these decisions. The Central Bank was unpopular with the government due to its opposition to the hard-line on IPC, and also because of its close association with Valdivia. Some members of the Bank were also accused of leaking information to the opposition newspaper *Expreso*.[37] In the commission, one of the Bank's high officials was asked for his opinion of the Toquepala contract.[38] He replied that this had nothing to do with the enquiry, and he then lost his job. The head of EPF, Sr Ferrand had earlier been associated with a suggestion that the Talara complex should be turned into a joint venture between IPC and the state. Ferrand was not only a man of the Right, but also a civilian in a job which, from that point on, was entrusted only to military officers.

As a consequence of these departures, Velasco was able to make new appointments, and thus to strengthen his position. Moreover, in early 1969, there was an administrative reorganization which gave him a further opportunity to promote his supporters. Thus, the Council of Ministers in April 1969 was:

Radicals and other Allies of Velasco	'Developmentalists'	Conservatives
Gen. Velasco	Gen. Montagne (Prime Minister)	Vice Adm. Navarro (Navy)
Gen. Artola (Interior)		
Gen. Arrisueño (Education)	Gen. Mercado Jarrín (Foreign Minister)	Gen. Benavides (Agriculture)
Gen. Fernández Maldonado (Energy and Mines)	Gen. Morales Bermúdez (Finance Minister)	Rear Adm. Camino (Industry and Commerce)
Gen. Meza Cuadra (Transport and Communications)		Rear Adm. Vargas Caballero (Housing)
A. F. G. Gilardi (Aviation)		
A. F. G. Chamot (Labour)		
A. F. G. Montero (Health)		

[37] By *Oiga*, 14 February 1969.
[38] Personal communication from Shane Hunt, 16 August 1974.

Of the new appointments, two—Fernández Maldonado and Meza Cuadra—were radical Colonels who had played a major part in the coup, and subsequently joined Coap. Fransisco Morales Bermúdez had been promoted General in 1968. He had been widely suspected of plotting a coup along with General Dóig Sánchez in early 1968 but he then decided to join Belaúnde's government as Finance Minister. This was a miscalculation; he made enemies in the military by deciding to join the Cabinet, and enemies among civilians by deciding to resign from it soon afterwards. Thus, he did not figure in the first military government. His re-emergence may have owed something to his personal friendship with several radicals—including Fernández Maldonado and Meza Cuadra. At the same time, Morales was suspected, in at least some quarters, of radical sympathies in a way amply disproved by later events.[39] Finally, the participation of the navy in the government was expanded by the addition of two relatively conservative figures—Vargas Caballero and Camino—who may have been selected by Navarro.

Even then, however, the overall political direction of the government was still unclear. The Council of Ministers was still a coalition, admittedly one whose balance had shifted markedly to the Left in the six months after the coup itself, but it was still true that decisive action would only be possible after agreement had been reached between officers of potentially diverse political orientation. Perhaps in order to minimize these difficulties while the government consolidated its position, Velasco quickly embarked upon an extremely aggressive series of nationalist initiatives, mostly directed against the U.S.A. Thus, the final takeover of IPC coincided with Peruvian recognition of the U.S.S.R. and the countries of Eastern Europe; a trade pact with the Soviet Union was also signed in early February 1969. Later the Peruvian government, rejecting a series of political initiatives by the U.S.A. which were aimed at securing some kind of compromise solution to the IPC dispute,[40] embarked on a diplomatic initiative to secure the

[39] For example, by *Caretas*, 12 April 1969.
[40] In June 1969, C. Roper wrote that the Americans 'have agreed to forget the whole affair if the Peruvians will make a token payment of US $2m. to close the account'. 'Peru's long-standing Problems' in *The World Today*, June 1969, p. 254.

support of other Latin American governments in the event of a confrontation over the issue. Foreign Minister Mercado also tried to increase the pressure on the American government by hinting at a decisive radicalization in Peru if the Americans did apply the Hickenlooper amendment (which provided that American aid should be cut, and the sugar quota cancelled, in the event of any Latin American country refusing to pay compensation for nationalized American property). As Mercado himself put it, 'We all remember what happened in Cuba'.[41]

The Peruvian government also raised another irritant in Peruvian–American relations by enforcing the Peruvian claim for a 200-mile fishing limit. Indeed in February 1969, an American fishing boat was fired on, and several others were seized and heavily fined for illegal fishing. In retaliation, the American government cut off military aid to Peru, and the Peruvians replied by expelling the American military mission in Lima. In May 1969, a further worsening of Peruvian–American relations occurred when the Peruvian government refused to receive Governor Rockefeller (who was on a fact-finding mission to Latin America) in Lima.

Despite these differences, however, confrontation never became total. In the event, the American government did not apply the Hickenlooper amendment, in a decision which was seen as a victory for Peru. Instead they imposed a quieter and more limited financial blockade which (as we shall see) eventually posed serious problems for Peru.[42] Nevertheless, the immediate decision, first to postpone, and then to suspend, the application of the Hickenlooper amendment appeared to be a complete vindication of Velasco's position.

Thus, by the middle of 1969, the forces behind the October coup had established powerful positions in the military government. Velasco had been able to consolidate his own coup. A number of key cabinet posts were now held by his strong

[41] *Financial Times*, 25 February 1969.

[42] Einhorn described U.S. economic pressure thus: 'The policy when implemented, came down to U.S. government denial of Export-Import Bank credits to businesses seeking investments in Peru, no new AID authorisations, and a policy of preventing loans, insofar as possible, from going to Peru from the international financial organisations. The policy was part of a negotiating scenario which suggested doing everything you possibly could without having to admit it. If something came up that would force an admission, then give in.' J. Einhorn, *Expropriation Politics* (Washington D.C., 1974), pp. 58–9.

personal supporters. The 'radical Colonels', now become Generals, had also achieved a solid position of influence. This became even greater after the replacement of Benavides by General Jorge Barandiarán in June 1969. Nevertheless, the radicals' position was never securely dominant. There were always a number of moderate officers within the government occupying influential positions. The political implications of this diversity will be examined in subsequent chapters, but first it will be useful to examine the attitudes within the government and among its civilian supporters.

Differences within the Military Government

While there are always problems with terminology, the most useful division of the military government appears to be into 'radicals' and 'developmentalists'. One dimension of this difference in mid-1969 was explained by Cotler in the context of the agrarian reform.

These ideologies can be broken down into two basic points of view; one emphasises change in the relationships of power, while the other sees the axis of change in the problems of production and productivity. The first considers that only a redistribution of resources among the marginal population will achieve an increase in the capacity for consumption which will, in turn, increase production. The second position proposes an increase in the productivity of enterprises through their capitalisation, the progressive economic incorporation of the population and an increase in consumption. The problem of economic concentration, and the consequences derived from this position, attacked by the reformists, are, according to its supporters, political and not technical arguments.[43]

A 'change in the relationships of power' could, of course, occur in several different ways. In a destructive sense, it was clear that such a strategy would mean that the wealthy and seemingly powerful oligarchy and foreign companies would come under attack. Indeed, an attack on the oligarchy would win independent support within the army as a whole. This immediate emphasis on attack, however, disguised a major difference in emphasis between those whose main interest lay in a transfer of

[43] J. Cotler, 'Political Crisis and Military Populism', in *Studies in Comparative International Development*, vol. 6 no. 5 (1970–1, pp. 95–113), p. 105.

economic power to 'the people', which, in practice involved various kinds of experiments with co-operative ventures and worker self-management, and those who wished to set up a strong state to encourage a national capitalism. Thus, whereas the military radicals would later call themselves socialists (although of the Christian rather than the Marxist kind), the 'developmentalists', who commanded a great deal of support within the army, were fundamentally pro-capitalist even though they wished to carry out a number of pressing structural reforms. Indeed, although this division was only implicit at first, it came, as we shall see, to have a major impact on the future of the military government.

However, for quite some time it appeared that differences within the government after mid-1969 reflected shifts in emphasis rather than clearly defined ideologies. Thus, it seemed as though some ministers were basically concerned with reform (that is, with the expansion of the role of the state and the development of new kinds of participation), but did not wish to damage the economy or the political base of the government, while others, willing to go along with reform, were more concerned with political and economic stability, and perhaps also with civil liberties. In any case, both of these tendencies opposed IPC and the oligarchy and called for sweeping reforms. At the time, this seemed to be a sufficient base of unity and the extent to which the government was divided over fundamentals was not immediately clear. Thus, until around 1973, relationships within the Council of Ministers remained fairly amicable, with policy being made by a process of internal compromise and bargaining. Until then, the President found it necessary to live with both tendencies, and they with him.

Civilian Attitudes to the Military Government

Many civilians were taken by surprise, both by the coup itself and by the growing radicalization at the beginning of 1969. Inevitably, therefore, there was a period of confusion during which certain families and interests which had initially supported the regime became increasingly alarmed by it, while others, who had originally opposed the military intervention, felt a growing need to accommodate themselves to it. In fact, apart from the old oligarchic interests (which were liquidated during 1969 and 1970), most groups which had been active in pre-1968 politics had at least some access to the military government. For the regime, however, such accessibility posed severe problems; it could hardly refuse all contact with those who had genuine economic power, but, if it maintained such contacts, these might threaten its own unity.[44]

It was certainly true that competing interests sought to cultivate different military and governmental supporters. Thus, the military radicals provided a focal point for the support and the advice of the civilian Left, some of whose members came to occupy influential posts within the government. The more radical line was also supported in the press by *Oiga* and (after its expropriation in March 1970) by *Expreso*. The 'developmentalist' officers could count on the support of *El Comercio*, as well as the private business sector and the managers of certain of the nationalized industries.[45] It is not surprising that the advice and influence of these groups tended over time to pull leading members of the regime in different directions. As we shall see in the next chapter, however, Velasco was not without resources when it came to securing unity within the military and within the government.

Conclusions

The transformation of the internally divided military government of October 1968 to the far more nearly homogenous

[44] The internalization of conflicts existing within society is widely believed to have been important in destroying military unity in several other cases. Thus, Gallo once noted of Argentina, 'To put it briefly, the armed forces have been subject to the same sort of pressures that have harassed the civilian administrations. The various pressure groups that operated through Parliament in periods of constitutional rule started to use competing factions of the armed forces to achieve their aims. The result has been a highly politicised military body in which generals and colonels played roles similar to those performed by deputies and senators in normal political times. All these struggles severely weakened the authority of the military regimes, and forced them to call for a return to constitutional practices.' E. Gallo, 'Argentina; background to the present crisis', *The World Today*, November 1969, p. 500.

[45] The influence of the press and business associations upon the regime are discussed more fully in chapter 7 of G. Philip, op. cit., and see also J. Fenner, 'The General as Revolutionary', in the *Columbia Journal of World Business*, May 1970; T. Utley, 'Doing Business with Latin American Nationalists: the case of Peru', in *Harvard Business Review*, March/April 1973, and C. Goodsell, op. cit.

regime which consolidated its position in mid-1969 was very clearly due to the political situation in which the military found themselves. Once the coup had taken place, it had to be justified in terms of action in order to maintain a sense of purpose within the officer corps and thus to prevent dissident officers calling for a return to civilian rule. The most obvious justification that existed lay in Belaúnde's failure to deal firmly with the International Petroleum Company. Within the military itself, nationalism also presented an excellent tactical opportunity to the military radicals. The hard-line which Velasco took over IPC emphasized the divisions among the military conservatives, and so prevented them from combining against him. It also enabled Velasco to remove just enough prominent conservatives to tip the balance of power within the Council of Ministers in his favour. Moreover, the aggressively nationalistic policies which he pursued through early 1969 helped to distract attention away from the purge of *entreguistas* and from the administrative reorganization which finally placed his own supporters in key positions.

As we have seen, this radical nationalism, which the military government expressed in its early conflicts with IPC, was deeply rooted in a set of values that had taken an increasing hold on the Peruvian army during the 1960s. In order to triumph, these ideas merely needed a promising tactical opportunity, and this was provided by the Act of Talara. Such nationalist values could more easily be expressed when there was no threat from any kind of radical civilian organization, because then the conservative counter-argument—that nationalism encouraged subversion—lost much of its effectiveness.

This early victory over IPC, however, was not enough to allow Velasco to create a Council of Ministers that was wholly in his image. In fact, the government has never been a homogenous entity, singlemindedly pursuing a specific set of objectives. Even after the resignation of Benavides in mid-1969, important differences remained within the government. Its most radical members were 'Velasco's Colonels' who had, by mid-1969, taken over several important ministries. This group wanted the military government to bring about a complete transformation of Peruvian society, including comprehensive reforms in almost all areas, and the definitive elimination of the old bases of political power. Velasco himself appears to have supported most of these aims, albeit more circumspectly than some of the more junior ministers. A second group of 'developmentalists' also remained. These had supported Velasco over IPC, and were willing to support extensive reform (albeit with less enthusiasm than the radicals) but were concerned with its effect on economic and political stability and opposed to full-scale socialism. The genuine conservatives, however, were for the time being either eliminated or forced to go along with the reform programme and act as 'developmentalists'.

IV
THE VELASCO GOVERNMENT AND THE OFFICER CORPS, 1969-73

Velasco's government, as it emerged in 1969, showed itself willing to confront the most prominent civilian groups and classes within Peru, not only the oligarchy, but also much of the middle class and all of the previously influential political parties and organizations. Although it also looked around for civilian political support for its objectives, its immediate, and also its ultimate, political base rested within the officer corps itself. As we have seen, there were good reasons for believing that this base, at least in the first instance, might be capable of sustaining considerable pressure provided that it was effectively managed. For the first four years at least, this criterion was fully met.

The immediate problem for the military radicals was that of maintaining the loyalty upon which they had so far relied successfully. Their ability to do this depended on two factors; military potential for unity, and the radicals' ability to convert this potential into actual support. We have already seen that military potential for unity in Peru was considerable and growing,[1] and it may be useful to stress again some of those factors which brought this about.

Background Features

One of the most striking features of the Peruvian military was its relative isolation from the civilian elites, and even middle-classes. In fact, there is always some gap between the military and society, based upon the differences in lifestyle and career prospects between officers and the civilian middle class. For these reasons alone, military 'self-images' are likely to differ from those of civilians. Thus, in Peru, military 'discipline' and separation from civilian life have been regarded as virtues. According to Einaudi,

[1] See above, pp. 40-5.

because discipline is a virtue restricted to the military, officers who have frequent and continuing contact with civilians run the risk of contamination, of losing their discipline, and of no longer being sufficiently military in the eyes of their colleagues. Activities involving civilians must therefore constantly be evaluated by the standard that they are tolerable only 'so long as they do not impair the discipline and efficiency of the armed forces'.[2]

Moreover, there is a clear difference in social origin between military officers and civilian elites in Peru. Typically, army officers came either from military families (in such cases as Montagne, Morales, Benavides and the Barandiarán brothers) or from the provincial lower middle-class (such as Velasco himself). Even more important in 1968, however, may have been the general lack of participation by military officers in industrial or agricultural management. Thus, according to Einaudi,

of the 630 men who in 1963 belonged to the boards of directors and top management of the 86 largest business enterprises in Peru, only four were military men, and the only ones, as far as can be determined, ever to have served in the military. Of these four, one retired general, and one retired colonel, were presidential appointees on the boards of semi-public corporations; another was an active-duty colonel serving as an adviser to the board of an explosives company ... None of the 52 members on the board of the National Agrarian Society in 1963 was a military man, although one had a brother who was a military officer. Similarly, fewer than one per cent of the exclusive *Club Naciónal* were military officers.

Therefore,

Peruvian officers, in part because state enterprise has not been extensive in Peru, have had relatively little experience in economic management. This means that their perceptions of business problems and potentials is more limited than, for example, that of their opposites in Argentina and Brazil, who, for many years, have been involved in various kinds of state controlled or managed business organisations.[3]

To this isolation must be added the effect of ideology. It has been noted in other contexts that ideology can powerfully reinforce group self-consciousness and thus capacity for united

[2] Einaudi, 'Changing Patterns...', p. 13.
[3] Einaudi, ibid., p. 42.

action.[4] Indeed, it is generally accepted that ideology contributed much to the strength of Communist parties even when —as in Russia under Stalin—the ideology was only tenuously related to actual government policy. Similarly it is likely that Caem ideology, even where not particularly original or profound, added a modern 'technocratic' form of legitimacy to what was already seen as a military right to rule. The claims of martial virtues, political effectiveness and technical expertise could then work in the same direction, as Velasco made clear when he declared that 'our role as governors is inseparable from our role as military officers.'[5]

Political Organization

(A) EXTERNAL

The regime, however, did not need to rely on authority alone. It had also, by 1968, evolved a style of government that deliberately aimed to remove officers from civilian influence through the construction of a purely military government, organized according to military as well as political criteria. Thus military and governmental hierarchies were no longer separated, and troop commands provided a stepping stone on the path to political office. Moreover, in a determined attempt to reduce the danger of factionalism, the government kept independently-influential civilians well away from real power—even in advisory bodies and nationalized industries. The few civilians to reach high office before 1975 were, without exception, men without close ties to existing political parties.

The need to contain political divisions within the military also led to the imposition of increasingly rigorous press censorship as time went on. Indeed, in Peru, such censorship was particularly important because of the traditional influence which the press was able to exert over both military and civilian governments.[6] The first acts of repression took place almost

[4] See, for example, M. Schurmann, pp. 177–89, of A. Pizzorno (ed.), *Political Sociology* (London, Penguin, 1971).
[5] Quoted in *Nueva Cronica*, 22 December 1971.
[6] There is not yet any fully satisfactory discussion of the influence of the Peruvian press, but, for a discussion of the influence of *La Prensa* on the 1962–3 military government, see C. Astiz, *Pressure Groups* . . ., p. 147 et seq. The role of the press in the 1968–73 period is discussed in G. Philip, op. cit., pp. 258–61. For an insider's view of the Peruvian press, see the early chapters of P. Beltrán, *La Realidad Peruana* . . .

immediately and were directed against *Caretas*, which had been unusually outspoken in its discussion of the backgrounds and political positions of key members of the military government. Subsequently, early in 1969, '*Caretas* . . . reported and commented on a new "decree-law" enabling the government to summarily purge army generals who were out of line politically, as well as one of the four unpublicized pay rises that the military had received since taking power. The whole issue of *Caretas* was confiscated and its independent editor, Enrique Zileri Gibson, deported from the country.'[7]

Press freedom was curtailed even further with the passage of the restrictive Press Law, which was issued at the end of 1969. This threatened heavy penalties for very vaguely specified offences against the state, or against any individual, and thus effectively ruled out any open criticism of a government member or supporter. In February 1970, the regime went even further—responding to a strike at *Expreso* by nationalizing the newspaper and turning it over to various intellectuals who identified themselves with the Left-wing of the government.[8] Later in that year, *La Cronica* fell into the hands of the government after the bankruptcy of the Prado family. This was subsequently re-issued as a pro-government newspaper although it never achieved the same degree of influence as *Expreso*. As we shall see, in 1974 the regime went even further and expropriated the entire press—but in so doing it seriously over-reached itself and added to its difficulties. Until then, the government's main aims were effectively achieved by censorship.

(B) INTERNAL

Within the military itself a considerable degree of unity was made possible, and compatible with a reasonably effective process of decision making, by the adoption of an agreed set of policymaking procedures. While these undoubtedly involved a degree of informality, they were firm enough to provide procedural justification for the decisions made in particular areas

[7] N. Gall in *Dissent*, p. 310.

[8] *Expreso*, in fact, became one of the more vigorous newspapers, daring to attack the Fishmeal Law in March 1971 (for which it was sharply denounced by General Tantaleán, the Fisheries Minister) and later, in 1972, publishing an attack on Sinamos from members of a squatter settlement in Lima which faced relocation.

of policy. It is difficult to draw the line exactly between the formal and informal elements in the system, not only because of a simple lack of information, but also because the political leadership was concerned to present the policymaking process as formal and institutional even where the crucial decisions were taken by one or two powerful individuals. Procedural regularity, after all, suggests that those in formal positions do possess real power, and this may make decisions more widely acceptable. Regularity also gives a sense of security to military bureaucrats, who might otherwise be forced into defensive politicization in order to safeguard their interests. Thus, even blatantly political decisions were wrapped up, where possible, in the language of bureaucratic regularity; for example, the dismissal of Admiral Vargas Caballero in May 1974, which occurred because he had become the focal-point of Right-wing opposition to Velasco, was justified on the procedural ground that he had spoken on a matter (freedom of speech) which was outside the specific competence of his department.[9]

However, the policymaking process, both formal and informal, tended to centralize the making of decisions and thus to reduce the danger that the top leadership might lose effective control of the government machine. Broadly speaking, this centralization occurred as a result of the overlapping jurisdictions of government ministries and agencies whose disputes could be reconciled only at the top political level.

Thus, any important decision in the field of economic policymaking could only be made after at least three potential interdepartmental conflicts had been resolved. The first of these was between 'vertical' and 'horizontal' ministries. The 'vertical' ministries are those concerned with particular industries (such as Mines and Energy), and the 'horizontal' ones with general fields of operation (such as Finance). The Ministry of Finance, for example, and the Ministry of Mines and Energy shared the responsibility for securing foreign investment to develop Peru's copper mines, and (at least until 1975) the former took a con-

---

[9] Less than a year later, in March 1975, the navy had its revenge when Vargas Caballero's successor, the outspokenly pro-regime Admiral Faura, was forced to resign after he had made a speech defending the government, on the grounds that this was 'political' in character. This resignation finally destroyed Velasco's control over the navy and marked the beginning of the end for his regime.

sistently more accommodating line towards foreign capital than the latter. The second potential conflict was between the nationalized industries and the ministries to which they were nominally responsible; it was quite common for these conflicts to go before the Council of Ministers for resolution at the top political level. Finally, conflict often occurred between those organizations responsible for deciding overall policy (the Planning Institutes and the Presidential Secretariat) and those with specific departmental responsibilities. Under these circumstances, even when interest groups were able to 'capture' one particular government department, their influence would be checked by competition from other state sectors.

In order to reconcile this multiplicity of different viewpoints, there existed a fairly complex—but undoubtedly flexible—structure of decisionmaking.[10] Given this complexity, the key to the resolution of most disputes lay with the top political leadership; the President and Prime Minister. These were concerned with every issue, unlike the other ministers who theoretically at least were only expected to concern themselves with departmental matters. They also had the right to make statements about general items of policy, and did so frequently. A statement of this kind generally closed an issue. Moreover, while not much is known about the procedures for promotion and dismissal or of the way in which decisions were made within the Council of Ministers, it is likely that the President always had a great deal of power in these matters.

At least until 1974, therefore, Velasco had a great deal of personal power within the administration. His influence was pragmatic, generally discreet, but unmistakeable. As Lowenthal described him,

His skill in holding the military coalition together and assuring that discrepancies and divisions are kept internal is increasingly recognised, particularly after his sudden and severe illness in 1973 removed him from the palace temporarily. What is not so generally perceived is Velasco's own tendency to push for more extensive reform. His commitment to a sweeping agrarian reform, his personal desire to establish improved *rapport* with students, and his expressed concern

[10] 'Bureaucratic politics' within the military are discussed by P. Knight, in Lowenthal (ed.), op. cit., by D. Collier in chapter 7 of *Squatters and Oligarchs* ... and G. Philip, op. cit., chapter 7.

about educating the Quechua and Aymara-speaking populations—all seem directly to have influenced national policy. It seems likely that he has consciously led the Armed Forces towards policies most officers would have rejected in 1968 as too extreme.[11]

During Velasco's presidency, Coap provided another radical force within the military government. Coap, Velasco's personal secretariat, was initially set up in October 1968 and was composed of Colonels who had been active in supporting the coup, but who were too junior to move directly into the Council of Ministers. It appears to have retained its radical character throughout Velasco's presidency, and its most influential members seem to have been those who entered it at the beginning. Coap had the job of processing policy proposals from the ministries before they reached the Council of Ministers, and reconciling differences between them. In doing this, it was able to exercise considerable influence. Indeed, in several cases, it took the initiative on policy itself. Thus, according to Lowenthal,

from the start, Coap has played a major part in undertaking or revising some of the key reforms, often apparently against the opposition, or at least, without the active participation, of the relevant ministries.[12]

Just below this level was the Council of Ministers, which alone had the power to decree laws. Undoubtedly many departmental disputes could only be resolved at this level—generally by compromise but occasionally enforced. Under Velasco, when the Council of Ministers deadlocked on a major issue, a delay generally occurred while compromise was sought. The passing of the Industrial Law, for example, or the final nationalization of the daily press, occurred only after a long period of internal discussion within the government. In such cases, it was quite possible for dissident ministers to canvass openly for support outside the normal governmental channels (as Admiral Vargas Caballero did in mid-1973 over the issue of nationalizing *El Comercio*) although such a course might be dangerous if feelings ran high on both sides.

Below the Council of Ministers there was an extensive network of inter-departmental committees to process the recommendations made by particular departments. These were likely

[11] Lowenthal in *Foreign Affairs*, p. 813.
[12] Lowenthal, ibid., p. 814.

to resolve only the technicalities of any given proposal, but they also served as an *oubliette* for suggestions that were unacceptable at a given time, but of possible usefulness later. Thus, for example, the long-anticipated petroleum law never got beyond this stage.

Any particular decisionmaking process could be altered by legal changes to the jurisdiction of a department, or by changes in its personnel. Both of these offered the leadership real, but limited, opportunities for political control. This also appeared to be the case with recruitment to particular ministries, although not much is known in a formal sense about the procedures according to which government members were selected or dismissed; in fact, it is doubtful whether formal criteria existed. Nevertheless, under Velasco, there did exist 'rules' in the sense of consistent patterns of behaviour, which can be detected and which seem to have been important.

Departments, for example, with relatively few exceptions, were kept in the hands of particular services. The navy always kept the Ministries of Industry and Housing (as well as the Navy Ministry). The air force usually held the Labour and Health Ministries. The others, with certain exceptions, were kept in the hands of the army. Secondly, ministers were generally kept in the same position in the government. Exceptions occurred in a few, institutionalized, patterns of promotion (from INP or ONIT, to a full Cabinet position, or from a Cabinet position to the Prime Ministership or to one of the specifically military ministries) or in a very few cases when an officer was kept in a fairly junior position after retirement. Otherwise, retirement from active service also entailed resignation from the government, with the consequence that the 'natural' rate of turnover within the government was fairly high and the opportunities for any minister other than the President to create a personal following were limited. Moreover, while Velasco's health was good, he had the advantage over any of his challengers in that he had merely to maintain his position and wait for the officer concerned to retire.

Moreover, officers were subject to removal for failure. Certainly, there were also removals for what were obviously political reasons, but there was a long list of ministerial resignations that could convincingly be attributed either to specific blunders or to general ineffectiveness. In fact, some of the departed ministers, notably Leonidas Rodríguez from Sinamos in late 1973, were very close political allies of Velasco.

This set of procedures, therefore, afforded considerable opportunities for political control by the top leadership. Personnel, and departmental responsibilities, could at least to some extent be controlled. Moreover, the normal course of policy-making tended to create considerable numbers of interdepartmental conflicts. These widened the choices effectively open to the leadership by making it less likely that important issues would be decided at a lower level of the bureaucratic hierarchy. A system of this kind could work well, however, only when the leadership was strong, and, at the same time, willing to compromise and conciliate. Otherwise, if conflicts could not be resolved satisfactorily at the top level, the struggle for power among the heads of particular agencies would have disruptive effects. Open, uncontrolled competition for power at the top would inevitably tempt protagonists to look outside the government for support, and lead them to try to recruit the officer corps as a whole to a particular position. Political competition of this kind would clearly have a disruptive effect upon military unity.

It is also true, however, that an excessively autocratic President, openly using the weapons of political power against his subordinates, would have created serious problems for military unity in the long-run. Any attempt to ride roughshod over the opinions of high-level ministers could easily have led to a damaging series of resignations, which could, in turn, have disturbed the unity of the officer corps as a whole. This problem, however, is not limited to the military. In fact, cautious and conciliatory leadership tends to be necessary for a wide range of bureaucratic organizations, since the cost of conflict to their efficiency can be high. As March and Simon noted, open bargaining within an organization can be damaging since,

if those who are formally more powerful prevail, this results in a more forceful perception of status and power differences in the organisation. If they do not prevail, their position is weakened. Furthermore, bargaining acknowledges and legitimises heterogeneity of goals in the organisation. Such a legitimation removes a possible technique of control available to the organisational hierarchy. [namely that of ideological appeal].[13]

[13] J. March and H. Simon, *Organisations* (New York, 1958).

Moreover, a democratically elected President, with an independent source of legitimacy, can afford resignations in anger far more easily than a military President put into office by the support of his colleagues. At the top of the institutional structure, therefore, a very great deal depended upon the ability of President Velasco to manage a potentially diverse group of military officers.

This centralized but nevertheless cautious pattern of decision-making had a number of advantages from the perspectives of 'bureaucratic rationality'. The top political leadership had a considerable amount of influence over all decisions made within the bureaucracy, and could use this to minimize the disturbing influences of any inefficient, disruptive or dogmatic minister. Moreover, the need to maintain unity among potentially diverse military officers led the regime to pay particular attention to 'technical' arguments, in the hope that these would eliminate political differences within the officer corps and provide some common ground on which agreements could be made. As a result, expertise became a powerful bureaucratic weapon and the quality of the government's decisions may well have been improved in consequence.

These advantages, however, were inextricably tied up with an authoritarian political structure. All but the top leadership, and the few groups and departments directly concerned with any given field, were very firmly kept out of the policymaking process. Moreover, a structure of this kind could work well only when the leadership was strong and, at the same time, willing to compromise. Without such compromise, or under conditions of political uncertainty, there was a risk that political conflicts within the government might be exacerbated with a general increase in tension and the consequent 'politicization' of the officer corps. Under these conditions, the brittleness, which has been a feature of various other military governments, would become important in this one.

Military Organization
While conciliation and compromise were doubtless important, however, Velasco's government (like any other military regime) could also rely upon more direct methods of political control.

In Peru, as elsewhere, the judicious use of the resources of the state, and of military command, could greatly improve the prospects of any regime. Indeed, for a military government, the exercise of control may be particularly important, since the level of political cohesion in an army is likely to be lower than in, for example, a political party. Thus, questions of career prospects, salaries and so forth will be correspondingly more pressing.

Moreover, as Miguens points out,

writers, being intellectuals, tend to think that the officers who join a coup are motivated by political ideologies or affiliations. The real situation is very different. Officers, when they are not ordered to by their superiors, join coups motivated by a wide range of personal loyalties and ascriptive personal ties.[14]

The same is true, *a fortiori*, of why officers maintain an existing government in power. Thus, provided that he is popular, a senior general will normally be able to call on a wide range of personal contacts to help protect his position. Moreover, a small group of politically motivated officers (such as the leaders of the 1968 coup) may easily acquire a much wider, non-politically motivated following. This occurred in Peru. At various times such generals as Artola, Arrisueño and Tantaleán, although by no means radicals, undoubtedly helped to protect Velasco's position.

Moreover, the leaders of the 1968 coup took very good care to put their own men in command of key military positions. A few examples may help to illustrate this. Colonel Leonidas Rodríguez (promoted General in January 1969) was soon put in charge of the Lima division. He left this, in mid-1971, to enter the government, but returned at the end of 1973. Between 1971 and 1973 he was replaced by General Hoyos Rubío who, as a Colonel, had, on the night of the coup, been put in charge of the operation to arrest Belaúnde. Gallegos, another of Velasco's Colonels, was promoted General in 1969 and sent to command the 6th Division at Tacna. This crucial region was not only next to the Chilean border, but also to the Arequipa region, where the commander, a man of doubtful loyalties, was left strictly alone until his death in a helicopter crash in Novem-

---

[14] J. Miguens in *Studies in Comparative International Development*, p. 6.

ber 1973. After this, Gallegos moved to command the Lima Armoured Division.

The political leadership was also able to control a number of promotions. Not much is known about promotion mechanisms, but it would have been surprising if a military government had less control over promotions than its civilian predecessors.[15] Certainly the actual results of military promotions suggest that influential government figures had considerable discretion over who was recruited to join them, and who was maintained in particular positions after they had been appointed. Indeed, we have already seen how promotions in the navy and air force were manipulated immediately after the coup.[16] This pattern does not appear to have changed substantially during the Velasco government. Air Force General Gilardi, for example, was kept on as Minister of Aviation for six years, until his retirement, despite the fact that he was not particularly popular in (and was generally unrepresentative of) the air force. This has been attributed to the fact that Gilardi supported Velasco in 1968, when the latter's retirement was being discussed. Later, in May 1974, Velasco was able to sack Admiral Vargas Caballero for criticizing what he described as the over-sensitivity of the government to criticism. But this move, as we shall see, did have serious political repercussions.

Control over the army cannot be guaranteed simply by appointing troop commanders (as Goulart of Brazil found to his cost in 1964) but this is nevertheless an advantage. The Velasco government, however, not only determined troop commands, but also exerted the power of patronage over many jobs within the government bureaucracy. The great expansion of the state apparatus that took place since 1968 provided a powerful weapon of political control as well as attracting ideological support and the government was able to move particular officers into positions of responsibility simply by creating new jobs. While this expansion continued, rivalry over jobs could largely be contained, although eventual problems might have been inevitable once retrenchment became necessary.

Indeed, the scale of state expansion was very great indeed.

[15] On the civilian predecessors, see Astiz and Garcia, *Western Political Quarterly*, November 1972.
[16] See above, pp. 83–5.

This was true at the top level (where the Council of Ministers was expanded from 13 in 1968 to 18 in 1973, and where Coap, created for the first time in 1968, provided another twenty-five influential positions) as well as lower down. Indeed by 1974 the number of public corporations in Peru had increased from twelve to over forty, and by 1976 the number had risen to 179, accounting for some 120 000 employees.[17] Many of these provided at least one military job; Petroperú, the largest, at one time, provided five. All of these positions allowed officers to collect double salaries and many of them also offered considerable prestige and influence, while some less scrupulous officers may also have used them for direct personal advantage.[18] Moreover, within the military, promotions increased sharply in the aftermath of the coup, along with salaries and military decorations.[19]

Taken as a whole, therefore, these policies aimed at capitalizing on the strength of military self-awareness in order to create a new stratum of military bureaucrats which was armed, united and confident of its ability to lead Peru out of underdevelopment. While the financial cost of some of these measures was high, the military radicals were willing to support them in the hope that they would then be allowed a free hand to implement their proposals for the economic and social restructuring of the country as a whole. Like Allende in Chile, they tried to buy off potential military opposition, but—unlike Allende—they did

---

[17] *Andean Report*, September 1976.

[18] Corruption seems to have been kept under control until 1974. Nevertheless, stories do emerge. Thus, according to Gall (*Dissent*, pp. 309–10), 'When last May's [1970] earthquake occurred, a large expedition of military officers was in Mexico City at government expense to watch Peru play in the World Cup soccer matches. Ostensibly heading the delegation was General Artola himself, but when the earthquake broke, he could not be located, and finally was traced to a penthouse suite at the Hotel Lido in Miami Beach.'

In fact, the effect of corruption on political stability is ambiguous. On the one hand, it can enable political opponents to be bought off but on the other it can undermine solidarity (and stimulate jealousy among those excluded). Moreover, if disclosed, corruption can discredit a government. However, the military radicals, who appear to have been usually honest, were generally able (both in 1968 with the navy and in 1975 with a section of the army) to benefit from the corruption of others.

[19] On which, see Astiz and Garcia, op. cit. They state, for example (on p. 684), that in 1969 the military was still decorating Generals for parts played in the 1965 campaign.

achieve considerable success. For as long as the military institution was effectively led, it provided a base of support for the military radicals, but once Velasco's leadership faltered, the way would be open for his opponents to seek to control the state apparatus.

V
PROMISE AND PROBLEMS
1969-73

Even when Velasco's position was secure, he was never wholly able to disguise the fact that significant differences continued to exist within the government, even after the events of early 1969. These differences were not always clearly thought out, or even completely consistent, but it is nevertheless clear that there were two general tendencies within the regime. As we have seen, the developmentalists, who included such figures as Montagne and Morales Bermúdez, corresponded to the outlook of *El Comercio* and to the expectations of the Left.[1] These wished to carry out a limited 'modernization' of the economy, while at the same time intending to maintain a degree of popularity by adopting a nationalist image. Their opposition to the oligarchy stemmed from a belief that this was no longer in a position to contribute to Peruvian development, and they wished to give the state a greater role in pressing for industrialization. At the same time, certain kinds of foreign investment were still to be encouraged and the path of the more enterprising domestic capitalists was to be smoothed. These aims were substantially different from those of the military radicals, who included 'Velasco's Colonels'—Fernández Maldonado, Rodríguez Figueroa and the others—and could occasionally count on the support of Velasco himself. The radicals emphasized redistribution—of power as well as income—and thus supported worker participation, mass mobilization and extensive nationalization, although it is not clear how far they intended to manipulate popular demands and how far they were genuinely willing to respond to them. Certainly, their influential civilian advisers included some who aimed to mobilize the opponents

[1] While it can be exaggerated, there is a certain correspondence between the views of this group and those expressed by ECLA, as well as a certain similarity between it and the "positive left" of pre-1964 Brazil. In contrast, the radicals identified much more directly with the *dependencia* school, and their thinking is reflected in INP's *Plan Global* (vol. 1 of the 1971–75 *Plan*). See also pp. 95–6 above.

of the status quo and were willing to permit the demands thus raised to determine the regime's economic strategy.

Whatever the economic implications of these positions, the immediate difficulties which they faced were political.[2] As far as the developmentalists were concerned, even moderate reform might have been too much for domestic and foreign capitalists and might thus have raised the question of whether a military regime could manage a reformed capitalist state without the support of the capitalists themselves. Moderate reform also ran the risk of stimulating popular demands (and demands from within the military itself) for more drastic measures. Once reform began, therefore, the regime might be faced with a difficult choice between radicalization and reaction. Which would the developmentalists prefer?

In contrast, the radicals would face certain opposition from a variety of political groups—including the majority of the middle class but extending well beyond it. Any attempt to redistribute away from the urban sectors would be bitterly resisted, but—without such redistribution—it was difficult to see where the government's 'popular mobilization' could come from.[3] Nearly all of those groups who had benefited from the existing pattern of growth, and who had been able to exert economic power within it, had already been organized by civilian parties and would not welcome military radicalism. Moreover, any strategy aimed at redistributing income out of the proceeds of economic growth had to contend with the problem that any new growth pattern, even where successful, would create new vested interests and new opponents of redistribution. If the new pattern of growth was state-led, then this would merely mean that the new vested interests would be nationalized industries. In fact, the military radicals hoped that the expropriation of the oligarchy and a few major foreign companies would be sufficient to permit large-scale redistribution. As we shall see however they were disappointed.

Given this variety of view, major conflicts within the regime seemed inevitable and, as we have seen, it was widely believed

---

[2] The economic options open to the regime are explored in Fitzgerald, *State Capitalism.* . . . and in Thorp and Bertram, op. cit.

[3] In fact, as R. Webb pointed out (in Lowenthal, op. cit.), policies of income distribution under Velasco's four years differed little from those of Belaúnde.

that such conflicts would eventually prove decisive in undermining the government.[4] In 1969, however, neither of the tendencies within the government was clearly dominant, and neither had yet hardened into factions. Thus, the significance of these internal conflicts had not yet become fully apparent. For a considerable time the commonly held views on nationalistic self-assertion and economic reform appeared quite sufficient to guarantee a reasonable degree of internal unity. At first, this unity was reinforced by the regime's achievements. Thus, the Hickenlooper amendment was avoided, a sweeping agrarian reform was decreed and partially implemented, the banking system was largely nationalized and radical new laws were applied to industry, mining and fishing. During this time, it appeared that the sceptics had been confounded. The newly formed state enterprises achieved some impressive initial successes, and found credit from abroad surprisingly easy to acquire. So did the government as a whole. Indeed, in both 1972 and 1973, despite a limited American embargo on lending, Peru was able to borrow more from abroad in real terms than it had in any year under Belaúnde's government.[5] Moreover, the economic growth rate tended, if anything, to increase; apart from 1969 (when the recession could be blamed on Belaúnde), it did not fall below 5 per cent in real terms in any year before 1975. Indeed, despite its radical measures, the government even showed itself capable of attracting large scale foreign investment in both the oil and copper industries. It was no wonder that the 'Peruvian model' had such an impact on the rest of Latin America.

[4] See, for example, Einaudi, 'Changing Patterns...', as well as the discussion in the introduction.
[5] Growth rate statistics appear in Fitzgerald, op. cit., p. 64. Fitzgerald, together with Thorp and Bertram, op. cit., and G. Philip, chapter 5 of 'Policymaking in the Peruvian Oil Industry...' discuss the Peruvian economy between 1968 and 1973 in more detail. Peruvian financial statistics appear in the B.C.R.'s *Memoria* (annual) and *Cuentas*, 1960–73. A dollar price deflator appears in the U.S. Department of Commerce *Survey*. It should be pointed out, however, that this upsurge in international lending, while it owed something to prospects in Peru, responded to worldwide changes. According to the I.M.F. *Survey* (3 July 1973, p. 192) 'Having ample supplies of new funds, the Eurobanks had to look actively for new borrowers. As a result, they increased greatly their lending to developing countries'. However welcome this may have been for Peru, it left that country acutely vulnerable when the international climate changed.

At a political level the government's difficulties were more apparent. Even here, however, it was not clear whether its problems were anything more than the teething troubles normally associated with major changes. Moreover, the crucial element in the political model—the internal unity of the regime —survived. Indeed, Velasco's great personal ability to mediate between, and reconcile, divergent political perspectives was widely remarked upon.[6] Despite these appearances, however, it was during these early years that the seeds of the eventual crisis were sown. Overall, the government's political support was based upon perspectives that were too divergent, and the price of unity was consequently too high. Too often, the result of compromise was that no worthwhile goals could be properly pursued, and no valuable support could be won. Thus, expectations were raised but not satisfied. Fears were provoked and not properly assuaged. Opponents were created rather than eliminated. In the end the regime found that it had made enemies—but few friends.

The Agrarian Reform

The government's early legislation already embodied many of the ambiguities inherent in the regime. These could be seen, for example, in the Agrarian Reform Law of 1969. The principle of agrarian reform was itself barely controversial. It had enjoyed an honourable history—having been supported by President Kennedy during the early years of the Alliance for Progress, as well as by the military Junta of 1962–3 which had enacted the first agrarian reform law in Peru. Indeed, as we have seen, most Peruvian politicians paid lip-service to the principle of agrarian reform, although few were eager to undertake decisive action in practice.

Extension of the reform programme from the Sierra (where it had already, if somewhat ineffectively, been established in the Law of 1964) to the exporting *haciendas* of the North Coast was more ambitious. Even here however, the case for reform was strong. In the eyes of the Left, and of the military radicals, the oligarchic families which drew their primary source of

[6] See, for example, Lowenthal's articles in *Foreign Affairs*, 1974, and in *Continuity and Change* . . .

income from these *haciendas* were responsible for Peru's conservative economic policies and general underdevelopment; indeed, in the eyes of the radical officers, the 1968 coup had been directed against the oligarchy. For the developmentalists, the case for reform had become persuasive as a result of the poor growth rate of agricultural production; this had risen by an annual average of only 1.5 per cent between 1960 and 1969— in real terms—compared with an estimated population growth rate of 2.9 per cent per annum. It was widely believed that an agrarian reform which expropriated the coastal *haciendas* and so prevented the transfer of capital from agriculture to commerce and real estate, would increase agricultural productivity. It was also hoped that, by allowing a redistribution of income within the sector, reform would also stimulate domestic industry. Moreover, there were also political arguments for reform: for the developmentalists there was the promise that, by remedying just demands, it would take the heat out of peasant unrest (which had been a nuisance, though hardly a matter of great concern, to Belaúnde's government),[7] while for the radicals reform offered an opportunity to compete with the Apristas for popular support in the 'solid North'.

While these arguments were strong, however, they were not immediately effective. The appointment of General Benavides, a well known military conservative, as Minister of Agriculture in October 1968 seemed to guarantee that the government would not press for a drastic agrarian reform. Indeed, Benavides soon clashed with the radical colonels in Coap when the latter began to press for a new agrarian reform law.[8] Benavides did expropriate some of the lands belonging to the Cerro de Pasco Corporation under the law of 1964, but he continually resisted any attempt to replace this extremely insipid measure with anything that would have affected the coastal plantations. Not even the defeat of General Valdivia at the beginning of 1969 appeared to shake his position. In June 1969, however, Benavides suddenly resigned over a government decision to control

[7] Indeed, according to Bell ('The Politics of Agrarian Reform in Peru, 1972–6; the CCP and the CNA.' mimeo, London, February 1977) and to Handelsman (*Struggle in the Andes* . . .) the Belaúnde government was quite successful in heading off radical opposition in the Southern Sierra, where most of it was concentrated.
[8] See *Caretas*, 14 October 1968.

the level of domestic food prices. Within a week of his resignation, the agrarian reform law was promulgated.

In fact, the decisive impetus to the new law was provided by an outbreak of student rioting in the Sierra in protest against a recent education measure which reduced the political power of students in the making of university decisions. This violence allowed the radicals to regain the initiative by arguing that a sweeping agrarian reform would ultimately reduce social tensions. As Cotler recounted,

with regard to the violence at Huanta, the Minister of Energy and Mines, a well known developmentalist [i.e. radical] made public statements in terms of the identity of interests between the students and the Armed Forces, in the sense of producing changes that would drastically affect the social structure. The law of agrarian reform, which had been under study, was passed after an uninterrupted debate which last 15 hours... Eight enterprises controlling approximately 90% of sugar production were taken over the day after the passage of the law.[9]

The speed with which the largest coastal plantations were taken over was certainly impressive, and it clearly showed the motivation behind the measure; the aim had been to attack the sources of economic power rather than to undertake the slower process of increasing productivity in the backward parts of the Sierra.[10] However, even within the context of the North Coast, there were serious ambiguities in the government's programme. Was its main aim to increase production, as the developmentalists believed, or was it primarily intended, as the radicals hoped, to redistribute income and generate political support? The tone of the law was certainly moderate; according to one authority, 'the overall strategy was to strengthen commercial farming, preferably through the cooperative organization of small peasants, in order to increase the marketable surplus and expand the market for industrial goods.'[11] The speech in which

[9] J. Cotler in *Studies in Comparative International Development, 1970–1*, pp. 106–7. On this, see also M. Valderrama, *7 Años de Reforma Agraria en Perú* (Lima, 1977), pp. 42–5.

[10] C. Harding quotes 'a top government official' as saying that the 'agrarian reform has begun in zones where there was a greater concentration of economic power, leaving treatment of the minifundistas until a later date', p. 19, *Agrarian Reform and Agrarian Struggle in Peru*, Working Paper no. 15, Centre of Latin American Studies, Cambridge, March 1974.

[11] Ibid., pp. 3–4.

the law was proclaimed, however, was impassioned and radical.[12]

Indeed, peasant expectations were greatly aroused both by the passage of the law and the tone of the speech.[13] Consequently, in view of the absolute shortage of cultivable land in Peru, and the relative shortage of economic resources (since this was not intended to be an expensive reform), the law directly involved the government in a large number of almost intractable disputes throughout Peru.[14] While these cannot be fully described here, they may be categorized into those involving disputed claims for land and those involving conflicts with the economic technocrats over the allocation of surplus from the agrarian co-operatives. In the former type of dispute, government agencies had to choose between steadfast support for one particular claim or interest, thus antagonizing all the others, and vacillation or compromise, which, in a highly charged atmosphere ran the risk of antagonizing all sides. In the latter type, the government was, quite simply, an opponent; it could choose between intransigence, which was particularly dangerous in the Northern *haciendas* where the permanent workers had real power, and surrender, which would win few active friends, and which would annoy the regime's economic planners and end any prospect of full scale income redistribution to other rural workers.

Thus, although no cataclysm occurred over the reform (local conditions varied far too much in Peru for this to have been a serious possibility) there did occur an increasingly troublesome

[12] One of Velasco's sentences read 'Today, the day of the Indian, the day of the peasant, the Revolutionary Government is making the best of all tributes to him by giving the whole nation a law which will end forever an unjust social order'.

[13] See Handelsman, op. cit., and the chapters by Harding and Scott Palmer in Lowenthal, *Continuity and Change* . . .

[14] According to C. T. Smith (p. 93 of 'Agrarian Reform and Regional Development in Peru', in Miller et al., *Social and Economic Change* . . .), 'careful calculations have been made of land available for distribution in the light of the dispositions made in the agrarian reform law and these quite clearly point to the sad fact that there is nothing like enough land to go round. Indeed, it was concluded that there was land enough only to give satisfactory holdings to 14 per cent of qualified candidates in the two major zones, the coast and the Sierra, affected by land reform.' Apart from this chapter and the references in note 13, see Valderrama, op. cit., and Bell, op. cit., for a discussion of the politics of the land reform.

series of local disputes which, at times, aggravated conflicts of a different nature.[15] Thus, in late 1973, the whole of Southern Peru was shaken by an outburst of rioting in which rural discontents became temporarily fused with teachers' and students' riots. Moreover, the raising and partial disappointment of expectations by the reform strengthened, rather than weakened, the opposition groups—APRA on the Right and the CCP on the Left.[16] Not surprisingly, therefore, agricultural production continued to grow less rapidly than population.[17]

The most immediately dramatic series of conflicts took place in the most technically advanced sector of Peruvian agriculture —the exporting *haciendas* of the North Coast. It was here that the reform concentrated its early force—in order to destroy the oligarchy and to discredit the Aprista trade union leaders who had been central to that party's strength. The destructive aims of the reform were accomplished quickly enough, but the reconstruction of a new order proved infinitely more difficult, and was only possible when Aprista leaders were permitted to reappear under another name. From the beginning there were serious conflicts between the economic managers appointed from the centre, and the organized workers who sought to benefit directly from the end of private ownership. Indeed, soon after the law was promulgated, the technocrats, who had become increasingly worried by the government's rhetoric,

[15] The de-radicalizing effect of Peru's diverse regional geography has been widely noted. Thus, even APRA and Acción Popular had to rely on political support which was largely regionally based and, even within each region, local rivalries often inhibited reform organizations. See, for example, E. Dew, *Politics on the Altiplano: the dynamics of change in rural Peru* (Austin, Texas 1969). Simple ignorance of local conditions, however, was also a great handicap for the government. Thus, according to Roberts, the government agency Sinamos, could in Huancayo 'devise no framework to make for consistent policy: in many instances which we recorded, these officials were manipulated by local interest groups. [Consequently] the ambitious programmes of Sinamos had little success and were, in some respects, creating problems for the government by arousing antagonism at the local level', p. 185 of Miller et al., *Social and Economic Change* . . ..

[16] As well as representing the coastal plantation workers, APRA had the support of many medium-sized farmers worried (as it turned out, justifiably) that the minimum 'unaffectable' landholding might be reduced. The CCP (Confederación de Campesinos del Perú), which was led by Marxists, was able to win support from those who felt that they had been left out by the reforms.

[17] See Fitzgerald, op. cit. Agricultural growth rates were 7.8 per cent (1970), 3.0 per cent (1971), 0.0 per cent (1972), 2.4 per cent (1973) and 1.8 per cent (1974).

'threatened to paralyse production by resigning *en masse*, immediately before the scheduled formation of worker cooperatives'.[18] Partly as a result of this protest, the government decided to appoint an officer from Army Intelligence to each co-operative and to appoint the members of the co-operative commissions. Not surprisingly, these measures, and their economic consequences, triggered off a series of strikes from the Aprista-led workers that seriously disrupted production.

The outcome of this conflict was a clear victory for the unionized workers who succeeded in establishing themselves as an island of privilege within a sea of rural poverty. The government, after several attempts to repress them, was eventually forced to back down. The radical Minister of Agriculture resigned in mid-1971, and effective responsibility for the coastal estates was subsequently transferred to Sinamos (a new government body which was formed in 1971). This did succeed in calming the disturbances, but only did so by making concessions. Free elections were held in the co-operatives, and well-known Apristas were allowed to take office. Meanwhile, serious attempts to redistribute income to the rest of the rural sector were sharply curtailed.[19]

While this outcome was greeted as a success for the government (and for the newly-organized Sinamos), its long term effect was to emphasize the government's problems. Effective power within the co-operatives was held by non-government organizations (notably APRA) whose local leaders had led a successful revolt. By yielding in this, Sinamos may have brought peace, but it damaged two other government objectives—it gave up the attempts to undermine APRA and to redistribute income within the rural sector on a large scale. Moreover, this outcome implicitly raised questions that were subsequently to be discussed much more openly within the ranks of the military. Was it really worthwhile for the regime to seek independent sources of popular support? Might it not be better to abandon the attempt to create a distinctive base and instead to try to establish working relationships with existing parties? Might not

---

[18] D. Scott Palmer and K. Middlebrook, *'Military Government and Political Development; Lessons from Peru* (London 1975), p. 44.
[19] See Bell, op. cit.

a deal with APRA make it easier for the government to avoid serious civilian unrest?[20]

The Industrial Law
While these and other conflicts were played out in the countryside, the government turned its attention to other sectors of the economy. It was known, from early 1969, that the government was working on some kind of Industrial Law, but—despite a series of rumours which circulated during this time—it was not clear exactly what form the law would take until it was actually issued in September 1970. Indeed, despite the fact that it had only emerged after a long period of bargaining within the government, the essential provisions of this law had been a well-kept secret. Its appearance, therefore, was greeted with consternation by almost the entire private sector. The law itself was ambiguous in places (and was greatly 'clarified' subsequently) but its basic provisions were clear enough. These could be summarized under four categories. First, all 'basic' industries were to be reserved for the state. No new private investment would be allowed into these, and existing companies could gradually expect to be taken over, as indeed some were, by Induperú, which was set up in 1972. Secondly, private investment in other sectors was to be given various fiscal incentives according to a variety of criteria which included location, ownership and field of operation. These provisions were extremely complex and tended to create confusion. Thirdly, the law introduced certain 'fade out' requirements, after which all new foreign investment would revert to the state. The length of time which was to be allowed before such a 'fade out' became necessary would vary

[20] Haya offered his support to the government in a speech on his birthday on 22 February 1970, but this was refused, matter-of-factly by Velasco and later—more savagely—by Fernández Maldonado. However, this was not the end of the matter as we shall see in chapter 6. Moreover, according to *Marka* (20 May 1976) Artola in 1969–70 tried to persuade APRA to accept 'Aprismo without Haya' but was refused. Offers of this kind had been made before in Peru, and it was also in 1969–70 that the Argentine military tried (unsuccessfully) to create 'Peronismo sin Perón'. It is not known, however, whether Artola's initiative was purely personal, or whether it had wider support.

At a regional level, accommodation between APRA and the military was sometimes easier. Thus, according to *Latin America* (26 April 1976) 'in *La Libertad* [in the solid North], where all cane cutting is mechanised, the government has reached a comfortable accommodation with the APRA-dominated unions'.

according to whether the initial investment was a joint venture or was wholly foreign-owned. Finally, and most controversially of all, workers' 'Communities' were to be set up and given a right to a share in the profits and the management of each company; eventually, this share would reach 50 per cent and would thus permit workers to veto management initiatives.

This law, like that of the agrarian reform, appeared to provide a rather uneasy compromise between those members of the government who wanted to encourage private initiative and those who preferred to emphasize the primacy of the state, as well as between those who supported various forms of worker self-management and those who were reluctant to relax central control. Indeed, one observer described the outcome thus:

It is clear that Law 18,350 [the Industrial Law] represented a compromise which was able to satisfy men of differing political views. Those, such as Gens. Montagne and [Morales] Bermúdez who lean towards a neoliberal line, pressed hard for the inclusion of the sections which offered incentives to private capital; General Fernández Maldonado and his friends were able to include a clause which 'reserves basic industry to the state', the technical planners, interested in the social problem, obtained sections which established the intervention of popular sectors, and worker participation in the profits.[21]

Nevertheless, despite the nature of these compromises, the final shape of the Industrial Law had a great deal to do with the fact that the Industry Minister—Admiral Dellepiane—was one of the most radical in the entire government. Moreover, it is clear that the regime as a whole did not realize the effect that this law would have on the private sector.

In fact, the response was so hostile that the government was shaken. The main reason for this hostility was the uncertainty which had been created. The business community was completely taken by surprise by some of the most crucial provisions of the law. This lack of consultation was itself seen as an act of hostility towards the business community. Moreover companies were entirely unclear about the modifications, if any, that the government could be expected to make, and about the way in which the many vague provisions of the law would be inter-

---

[21] J. Petras and R. La Porte, *Perú ¿ Transformación Revolucionario o Modernización?* (Buenos Aires, 1971).

preted. Thus, the vagueness of the law came to be seen as a further threat, rather than as an opportunity for constructive negotiation with the government. Indeed, according to *Business Latin America* which was reporting shortly after the law was issued,

> to put it bluntly, most international companies already operating in Peru think that their days are numbered, and are looking to get out or cut back to a pilot light level of operation to maintain presence against the day when the situation improves.[22]

Of all of the concrete provisions of the law, by far the most unpopular among the business community was the *Comunidad*. This was intended partly as a sop to labour and partly as an attempt to win political control over it. The terms of the law explicitly sought to exclude workers connected with civilian political parties from playing an active role in the *Comunidad*, and it also tried to encourage workers to be 'moderate' by restricting the share of benefits paid out to workers who struck during the course of the year. At the same time, however, the law did hold out the promise of eventual power to the workers and, for this reason, was intolerable to most managers. Thus, a survey of 400 companies by the *Banco de Crédito* published in 1972 showed that 76 per cent of the respondents opposed the *Comunidad* concept (which, by then, had been considerably watered down) and only 10 per cent supported it. This was the bank's second survey. According to one source,

> the previous one, in 1971, was never published. The bank claims to have kept it off the press because it represented only a small sample, but the indications are that the response at that time was extremely negative towards the investment climate, and uncertainty over the government's legislation.[23]

In the face of these reactions, the more conservative members of the government began to reassert themselves. The Industry Minister resigned in mid-1971 and was replaced by a far more conservative figure. Subsequent regulations (and the Mining and Fishing Laws introduced in 1971) considerably watered down the *Comunidad* provisions. Indeed, highly desired

[22] 12 November 1970.
[23] Ibid., 6 February 1973.

investors, such as Bayer Chemicals, were allowed to avoid the power-sharing provisions altogether by undertaking joint ventures with the government; state undertakings were to be exempt from the power sharing provisions—these, after all, were generally managed by military officers!

As might have been expected, the eventual outcome of the law pleased nobody. Private manufacturing investment, already suffering from serious long-term problems,[24] fell away sharply despite the successive modifications which the government made to the terms of the original law. Meanwhile, the *Comunidades*, finding themselves offered only the shadow of power, felt betrayed and turned bitterly against the more conservative members of the government. Cotler described one incident thus

> In 1972 the Ministry of Industries convened the Congress of Industrial Communities. This assembly was of crucial importance, since it could have created a strong organisation which might have given important support to the government's programme.... In order to protect it from any kind of radical 'infiltration', the meeting was held at a military high school where the delegates and government officials were kept in seclusion throughout the proceedings. Outsiders were not allowed to enter the school, except by special permission of the sponsoring organisation.
>
> Despite these precautions, the delegates severely criticised the ministry's Department of Industrial Communities and ultimately forced the director of this department to resign. The criticisms were aimed at the failure of the ministry to respond to the numerous complaints made by industrial communities against businesses, which had found numerous ways to evade the provisions of the Industrial Community Law.
>
> While supporting the government's basic programme, the assembly moved to grant veto powers to community delegates vis-à-vis business management and later demanded that the government immediately transfer 50 per cent of the ownership of industrial enterprises to the industrial communities. These proposals were severely criticised in the official press... Subsequently the govern-

---

[24] On these more 'structural' problems, see Thorp and Bertram, op. cit., and Fitzgerald, *State Capitalism*... R. Webb also sought to explain the falloff in investment in 1969–70, which the government blamed on political factors, in terms of a demand recession (see *Caretas*, 16 May, 1970).

[25] Cotler, pp. 72–3 of Lowenthal, op. cit. See also G. Thorndike, *No! Mi General* (Lima, 1976). The assembly apparently had good reasons for taking this attitude.

ment decided to relegate to a minor role the Confederation of Industrial Communities.[25]

It is not surprising that, from the beginning of 1973, the Minister of Industry began to talk about 'reforming' the *Comunidad* system, while the private sector, beginning to recover its nerve, began to campaign with increasing openness against the whole concept.

Sinamos

Although the issue of popular involvement in the 'Revolution' was important to both the Agrarian and Industrial reforms, it was not the only objective pursued. The Agrarian Reform succeeded in destroying the economic power of the oligarchy while the Industrial Law (and a series of related measures, such as the nationalization of the major banks) did succeed in extending the role of the state in the economy. Thus, whatever problems were encountered by these laws, important 'technocratic' objectives were achieved. This significant, though limited, success made the more specifically political failures easier to bear. However, the same could not be said of the failure of Sinamos, whose objectives were solely political.

Ever since 1969, the radical wing of the government had been pressing for an organization to gather and crystallize support for the regime. The form which such an organization could take, however, was not immediately clear. The problem was that of pleasing all members of the government, despite their divergent political orientations, while at the same time holding out some prospect of success for the whole venture. Thus, it would be necessary to grant the new organization enough influence to induce independent civilians to associate themselves with it, but at the same time it could not be allowed to escape military control. Moreover, it had to act in a way that was compatible with other government objectives—it could not be permitted to engage in strikes against government owned enterprises, or agitations against government policy. Finally, it needed to be strong enough to compete successfully with its other potential rivals—the Apristas, the Communists, and the parties of the far Left. As it turned out, these requirements could not all be met.

The lack of a government organization, which accorded badly with the government's 'participationist' rhetoric, became painfully apparent in early 1970 when a series of 'Committees for the Defence of the Revolution' sprang up. These did not quite correspond to the Cuban variants, but they were nevertheless said to have been organized by the Communist party. Their emergence contributed to a major crisis within the government in March 1970, which only ended after military parades had demonstrated the loyalty of the army and after Velasco had embraced Montagne, who was earlier rumoured to be under house arrest. It is not known exactly what went on behind the scenes, but the 'Committees' ,after being given an initial welcome, were quietly discouraged.[26] At the same time, the programme of economic reform—which had also caused internal controversy—went ahead during the course of the year. It seems clear, therefore, that conservative military officers were more concerned about the danger from unregulated, possibly 'Communist inspired' political movements than about economic reforms.

The suppression of these 'Committees' made the organizational vacuum more obvious. Meanwhile, so far from countering the civilian Left, the reforms announced by the military government helped to strengthen it greatly. Thus, for example, the agrarian reform 'endowed the CCP with a legitimacy and a base of support which it had not known for over a decade'.[27] Moreover, pro-regime elements of the civilian Left were unable to provide a basis of support for the reforms since no kind of radical organization could survive unless it aggressively pressed worker and peasant demands. The CCP's success was due to its willingness to mobilize a variety of groups which could only be held together by a continuing series of protests and illegal actions.[28] Similarly, the Communist Party (which supported the regime and had been encouraged by the military radicals as a bulwark against APRA) found it necessary to embark upon an extremely aggressive series of strikes in the Cerro de Pasco

---

[26] R. Clinton, in IAEA 1971, quotes a rumour current at the time, that Velasco was forced to accept demands from a number of conservative officers in March 1970 that the 'Committees' be controlled, p. 53, fn. 2.
[27] Bell, op. cit., p. 8.
[28] Ibid., pp. 8–12.

complex which seriously embarrassed its military protectors, and led to the regime becoming far more repressive.[29]

In July 1971, therefore, Sinamos was created and put under the control of a noted military radical—General Rodríguez Figueroa.[30] It incorporated eight existing government agencies and organized them in a highly centralized way. It was given a fairly generous budget allocation (US$95m. in the first year) and virtually complete responsibility for local public works projects which it was to use in order to generate political support.

Sinamos, however, embodied rather than resolved the divisions within the government and the consequent ambiguities of government policy. Was it—as the more conservative officers believed—a kind of police agency, which might be a little more flexible than a purely military organization, but which was primarily concerned with 'law and order' and with making other government policies work? Or was it, as the military radicals and their civilian supporters hoped, an instrument of social mobilization and of generating mass support for the political line upheld by the military radicals? Organizationally, the conservative view appeared to prevail. From its beginning, Sinamos was closely tied in to the military hierarchy. According to one observer,

high ranking military officers were initially placed in charge of eight of the ten regional offices established by the 1972 organic law;

[29] On this see J. Ballantine, op. cit., chapter 5. *Oiga*'s tone towards the copper miners also changed sharply during 1971, when the most aggressive strikes took place, no doubt because it became increasingly aware of a conservative backlash within the regime.

[30] Some writers have seen Sinamos (and the Confederación Nacional Agraria, which was legislated into existence in May 1972) as evidence that ever since 1968 the Peruvian military government was pursuing a 'corporatist' strategy in order to head off pressure from below (see, for example, Cotler's chapter in Lowenthal, op. cit., and also J. Malloy, 'Authoritarianism, Corporatism and Mobilisation in Peru', *Review of Politics*, vol. 36, no. 1 (January 1974), pp. 52–84). This interpretation appears to fit in with a growing political science literature which emphasizes the repressive or 'corporatist' aspects of Latin American politics and it also connects with the regime's own counter-insurgency rhetoric. However, while there may well have been some long-term sense in which popular insurgency was feared, there was very little sign that this danger seemed pressing in 1968. Moreover, in those Latin American countries where the threat of revolt appeared real, the military reaction was correspondingly repressive. In Peru, the rhetoric of reform and participation was possible precisely because of the absence of such an immediate threat—and the 'corporatist' emphasis strengthened precisely when the regime's initial reforms began to run into trouble.

military officers or their close relatives were named to seven of the sixteen top positions in SINAMOS' national office upon its formal establishment in April 1972.[31]

Moreover, at a lower level, military influence was no less pervasive. According to Collier,

> The Sinamos program in the [Lima] settlements is closely coordinated with the armed forces in a way that enhances political control. It has already been noted that the armed forces have had a direct role in the settlements since the beginning of the period of military rule through their programme of levelling streets. The Organic Law of Sinamos explicitly reaffirms the role of the armed forces in settlement projects. The links between the armed forces and Sinamos go much further than this, however. Sinamos uses the army radio communications system to conduct much of its business in settlements ... the commander of the Lima military region is also head of the Tenth Region of Sinamos, the one that is concerned exclusively with Lima settlements. It is striking that this commander is in charge of the region that includes only the settlements, and not the region that includes the department as a whole.[32]

For these reasons, Sinamos never had serious prospects of becoming the means of revolutionizing the government's strategy. However, the publicity given to it, and its pervasive nature, quickly made it a target for intensifying popular demands, and, subsequently, for bitter frustrations. As a result, Sinamos was frequently plunged into situations which it could not control and, by its somewhat clumsy attempts at political manipulation (in this, it was no match for its civilian political rivals), it left itself wide open to damaging political attacks.[33]

At first, however, there was a honeymoon period. Sinamos did succeed in calming the turbulent sugar plantations of the North, but it did so only by making concessions. This apparent success, however, led Sinamos officials to become even more confident and to embroil the organization in a number of

---

[31] Scott Palmer and Middlebrook, op. cit., p. 22.

[32] D. Collier, *Squatters and Oligarchs* . . ., p. 108.

[33] Sinamos' problems may be compared with those of a related body—the CNA—which was set up in 1972 and held its first conference in 1974. The CNA, finding itself losing support to the opposition CCP (since 'it was apparent that only the CCP was able to mobilise the peasantry to force concessions out of the government'—Bell, op. cit., p. 10) decided to radicalize and compete directly with the Left. As a result, the agency was comprehensively purged by the regime, which was unable to tolerate conflict with its own supporters.

further disputes—over land settlement in the *barriadas*, over land tenure in the countryside, and even over trade union representation in the cities. But, as Sinamos' expansion grew, so did the reaction against it, thus,

in 1973 alone, Sinamos officers in Piura, Chimbote, Moquegua, Arequipa, Cuzco and Puno were occupied, sacked and/or burned by various striking groups—school teachers, construction workers, miners, fishermen, steel workers and peasants.[34]

In response to this antagonism, Sinamos' early idealism disappeared and it came increasingly to have the character of a (somewhat ineffective) apparatus of control. Thus, in September 1973, *Latin America* noted,

a mass exodus from the agency in recent months, particularly by younger personnel working in the field. In most cases, the regional offices of Sinamos are under the control of the local military or police commander, whose idea of what constitutes popular mobilisation and participation tends to differ radically from those of their younger civilian subordinates.[35]

The decisive blow, however, only came later in that year, when anti-Sinamos rioting shook Arequipa, Cuzco and a number of smaller Southern towns. This was only put down after full scale military involvement and the death toll, while never officially released, was considerable. After this, General Rodríguez returned to the command of troops and was replaced by a noted military hardliner; under his authority, Sinamos was quietly allowed to decline.[36]

Conclusion: The situation in 1973

By 1973, therefore, certain serious problems of the 'Peruvian model' had already become apparent. The most important of these was that military unity was coming to be threatened, not merely by the differences of outlook and perspective which are inevitable in any government, but by something altogether more fundamental. By 1973, nationalism and opposition to the

---

[34] Scott Palmer and Middlebrook, op. cit., p. 22.
[35] 7 September 1973.
[36] As Valderrama put it. Sinamos officials 'were scarcely to be seen' in the countryside after 1974, p. 32.

oligarchy were no longer enough to unite officers with very different ideas about how the country should develop. The 'easy' redistributions had largely been accomplished, but on their own they did not provide sufficient resources to enable the military to win over a political base. As we have seen, the land reform increased rather than reduced the political demands made upon the government, which did not gain much credit for reluctantly giving away what a variety of conflicting groups all believed to be rightly theirs. Meanwhile, the nationalizations of American property were possible largely because the expropriated properties (IPC, the Grace sugar plantations and associated industries, the fishmeal companies, Cerro de Pasco and a few other minor items) were not particularly profitable. If the expropriated groups were weaker than they looked, they were also poorer.

While the military had agreed on these targets, however, they had not counted on the opposition which they faced from the national 'non-oligarchic' bourgeoisie. This opposition and the lack of domestic private investment (which may, as was noted, have had much to do with non-political factors) posed a real problem for the military developmentalists. They could not create a domestic capitalism when the domestic capitalists obstinately refused to invest, but any attempt to grant incentives to this group would meet with the opposition of the *Comunidades* and, through them, of the radical officers. Moreover, it was not clear that a few modifications to existing laws, bought at a high political price, would achieve the desired effects. Rather, might not the removal of the most notorious military radicals offer the best possible inducement to the business community?

Meanwhile, the military radicals had problems of their own. The initial attack on the American government and the oligarchy had not had the hoped-for effect. On the one hand, the targets appeared to have crumbled too easily. CIA or oligarchic plots could always be denounced, but there was no sign of the public attack or open conflict which might have further radicalized the officer corps as a whole. On the other hand, the most unpopular targets had also been the least successful businesses. IPC and Cerro were barely profitable, while two of the most notable oligarchic families, the Prados and the Aspillagas, went bankrupt soon after the agrarian reform was promulgated. Thus, while the Peruvian government had now come into possession of some highly useful properties, these would only yield a return after several further years of careful investment. There could be no question of buying political support with the economic surplus. But if years of careful investment were necessary before the fruits of the Peruvian revolution became ripe, then what could be done in the meantime to meet the unrealistically high expectations of the government's potential supporters? Further redistribution could only be at the expense of the 'modern sector' as a whole, and would thus run counter to the developmentalists' hopes of strengthening national capitalism. But without redistributing imcome, how could the radicals succeed with their main objective—the redistribution of power?

VI

THE CRISIS 1973-76

In February 1973, a new dimension was added to the government's political problems; Velasco suddenly became seriously ill and the question of the succession was openly raised for the first time. This illness, and the two year period of uncertainty following his partial recovery, catalysed the conflicts within the government and accelerated its disintegration. Increasingly, internal problems which had appeared soluble or capable of compromise settlement were now a great deal more difficult. Power was much more overtly at issue than before, and the protection offered to the military radicals by their entrenched positions now seemed much less secure.

Indeed, Velasco's illness did not so much herald the arrival of new difficulties (although the economy became a source of increasing concern after around the middle of 1974) as emphasize the importance of existing ones. The need to choose between popular mobilization and the re-establishment of a modified form of capitalism became increasingly pressing until it led to the breakup of the coalition of 1969. In this breakup the radicals were defeated, and the developmentalist officers came to rely upon a rising group of military hardliners. Already by 1973, the existing coalition had come close to the limits of its unity; legislation now embodied reforms in agriculture, mining and industry and the basis of a large and powerful public sector had already been created. The question now was how to follow up these measures and make them work.

If nationalism had been central to the mood of the officer corps in 1969, then the question of law and order had taken its place by 1975. State control itself was barely controversial; in many cases, there seemed to be no credible alternative to nationalization while too many interests were now involved in the public sector for any kind of return to the pre-1968 economy to seem attractive. On the other hand, the rhetoric of opposition to the oligarchy and unchecked foreign penetration of the economy had now become slightly stale. In any case, with the government continuing to rely on large quantities of foreign finance, there were limitations on the extent to which this kind of radicalism could be pursued. Thus, by 1975, many officers had become convinced that the state should maintain its central economic role but that it should implement policy cautiously—at least until the financial situation improved decisively.

With state control becoming less important as an issue, the question of popular involvement in the revolution (or, conversely, of law and order) came to replace it. While the early reforms were being implemented, and the power of previously dominant interests was being destroyed, this question seemed subsidiary. Once existing structures had been demolished, however, it became increasingly necessary to face the issue of what to put in their place. Problems in this respect were even more acute because they were so largely unanticipated. The military radicals had assumed—in a manner similar to that of other authoritarian reformers—that they represented the real will of the people, not simply the 'national interest', and that the popular masses, once freed from their chains of exploitation through the measures which the military were introducing, would wish to do nothing more than support their military benefactors. The reforms were after all aimed at reducing, or even pre-empting, civilian rebellion by removing the grievances upon which rebellion could be based. Thus, the discovery that political conflicts remained, and even intensified, after the reforms was undoubtedly disconcerting, while the rough treatment meted out to government agencies under these conditions was even more so. These setbacks played into the hands of the hardliners of the Right who, after a period of eclipse, began to reassert themselves with the argument that reform encouraged instability, and that both needed to be avoided.[1]

This basic conflict intensified during 1973 and 1974. The military radicals, fearful of losing the initiative after the failures of Sinamos and the *Communidades*, badly needed a success which would again strengthen their position. They were keen to

[1] The beginnings of such a reaction were noticed by one observer as early as 1973. According to Einaudi (p. 417), military unpopularity was then already a problem and 'unrest, for whatever cause, is a sign of failure to accomplish a revolutionary goal, and thus it becomes a cause for pressure on the government'. L. Einaudi, 'Revolution From Within? Military Rule in Peru since 1968', pp. 401–27 of D. Chaplin, *Peruvian Nationalism*.

promote further reforms in the hope that they would eventually find the appropriate organization for stimulating suitable popular involvement. Nationalization of the press in 1974, and the social property legislation of the same year were both attempts to do this. Moreover, for a time, the military radicals were backed by Velasco himself who, under the impact of his illness, shed his previous conciliatory manner and became increasingly abrasive and personalistic.[2] Thus, such measures as the officialization of Quechua (which became a compulsory school subject, even in the middle-class suburbs of Lima), the nationalization of Gulf Oil and Marcona (which will be discussed below) and—above all—the repression of the weekly magazines which took place towards the end of 1974, all appear to have been implemented on the initiative of Velasco himself.

Meanwhile, the developmentalist officers, having achieved their initial reformist aims and now concerned with the problems of managing the new economic structure, became increasingly impatient with measures which seemed calculated to alienate groups whose co-operation was needed—such as foreign financiers, private businessmen and the new public sector entrepreneurs. Now that Velasco was ailing, these officers began to consider a new alignment with those openly conservative officers who had resisted reform from the beginning.

The first hint of such an alignment came with Velasco's illness in February 1973 when Mercado Jarrín, the Prime Minister, made a determined effort to take power. Mercado was a controversial figure. His ability was not in doubt; he had been an outstandingly successful Foreign Minister between 1968 and the end of 1971, when he had been promoted first to Army Chief of Staff and then to Prime Minister. As Prime Minister, however, he had proved to be a conservative and a hard-liner, politically close to the Navy Minister, Admiral Vargas Caballero, and to Admiral Jiménez de Lucio, who was Minister of industry.[3] His succession, therefore, was vigorously opposed by Velasco's own loyalists such as Fernández Maldo-

[2] After the coup, Morales Bermúdez justified his action in seizing power in terms of Velasco's 'cult of personality'.

[3] While it will never be known for certain, it would not be at all surprising if there was something personal, as well as political, involved in the rivalry between Mercado (who was a military intellectual and the former head of the Chorrillos academy) and Velasco (who was somewhat crude in language and lifestyle). In a

nado, Leonídas Rodríguez and Hoyos Rubío who at that time commanded the crucial Lima division. Perhaps even more important, however, Mercado was also unable to unite the non-radical officers, some of whom had political plans of their own, and who, therefore, had no interest in a quick succession. In any case, the situation was not yet critical enough for a sharp move to the Right to be attractive. Thus, both Morales, the Finance Minister, and Tantaleán, the Fishing Minister, refused to support Mercado. Consequently, as in 1969, the immediate effect of a leadership crisis had been to unite Velasco's supporters and divide his opponents.

Even so, if Velasco had died, it is difficult to see how Mercado could have been denied the succession without precipitating unmanageable internal conflicts within the military. As it happened, however, Velasco did manage a partial recovery and returned to the Presidency at the beginning of May, thus thwarting Mercado's immediate hopes. The situation was still difficult, however, since Velasco's supporters did not feel strong enough to remove Mercado from his position as Prime Minister, and the latter was not due to retire until the beginning of 1975. Thus, the only way for Velasco to defeat Mercado was by outlasting him. Consequently many officers were committed for at least eighteen months to supporting an invalid against a man whom they regarded as a threat.

The Nationalization of the Press

For some time the Peruvian government consisted of a sick President, a resentful and ambitious Prime Minister and a Council of Ministers which had divided openly over the issue of the succession. It was hardly surprising that the effect of these divisions came to be felt on other matters. An early conflict occurred over the appropriate government response to the strike at *El Comercio* in August 1973. *El Comercio* had initially been a warm supporter of the military government, but it had been progressively alienated by the regime's efforts to reduce the influence of domestic capitalists, as well as of the press itself. Moreover, subtly but unmistakeably it had identified itself with

country as socially stratified as Peru, it may well have been extremely irritating for Mercado to have to serve under a man from a lower-middle class social background.

the demands of the more conservative officers in the government, notably Mercado and Admiral Vargas Caballero. At the same time, the newspaper was a somewhat miserly employer, and had one of the poorest paid workforces in the entire Peruvian press. Consequently, when it was struck, it seemed at first as though the dispute was purely economic. The situation changed abruptly, however, when the workers called for its 'co-operativization'—as had happened with *Expreso* in February 1970. Indeed, *El Comercio*'s co-operativization was enthusiastically supported by *Expreso* itself, and backed by some of the military radicals. It was bitterly opposed, however, by such military conservatives as Mercado Jarrín, Morales Bermúdez and Vargas Caballero. Admiral Vargas Caballero, who played the most outspoken part in defending the existing ownership, was a prominent military conservative with strong support in the navy who had earlier strongly, but unsuccessfully, opposed the nationalization of the fishing industry. It was later said that Vargas Caballero had enlisted the entire navy in defence of *El Comercio*. At the time, this opposition seemed to prevail, and the matter was shelved, although A. F. G. Sala (an old ally of Velasco) was put in charge of a commission to look into the whole issue of press ownership.

Not long after Sala had taken charge of this commission, tensions returned as the radicals began to demand some kind of general press nationalization. The press, after all, might prove to be a powerful political weapon in what seemed to be a losing battle to mobilize popular support for the regime. Quite apart from the possibilities of censorship, the radicals would then be able to offer access to the media to their supporters. This would give the official organizations a powerful propaganda weapon in their regular struggles with Apristas, Trotskyists and other opponents of the regime.

In order to achieve nationalization, however, the military radicals first needed to deal with the increasingly confident Vargas Caballero and thus to isolate Mercado on the Council of Ministers (Morales, who had also opposed the expropriation of *El Comercio* in 1973, was spending 1974 as Army Chief of Staff, and so had no formal position in the government). The opportunity for this came in May 1974, when Vargas Caballero made a speech calling for greater tolerance on the part of the regime towards its critics. He was immediately sacked for making a 'political' speech, whereupon two of the other navy ministers in the government resigned with him. From then on, the navy became a centre of opposition to the regime and its position came to be supported increasingly by non-radical army officers and by important sections of the civilian middle class. The depth of navy resentment at this sacking can be gathered from the fact that Admiral Arce, who took Vargas Caballero's position, stirred up such personal enmity within the service that a number of other Admirals refused even to associate with him.[4]

After this incident, the way was open for the expropriation of the press, which took place in July 1974. This nationalization was swift and comprehensive. All the daily newspapers were taken over and editorial positions were given to civilian supporters of the regime. It was intended that, after a year of reorganization, the press would then be ready to be handed over to various occupational groups within the government's reformed economic structure. The way in which this was done can be seen from the following table:

Newspaper	Editor	Eventual Destination
El Comercio	Cornejo Chavez (Christian Democrat leader)	Agrarian co-operatives
Correo	Hugo Niera (ex-Sinamos official)	Professional organizations
La Prensa	Walter Penalosa (writer)	Workers Communities
Expreso	Ruíz Eldredge (pro-regime lawyer)	Educational associations
Nueva Cronica	Guillermo Thorndike (ex-Editor of Correo)	Government
Ultima Hora	Ismael Frias (pro-regime journalist)	Service organizations

Not surprisingly, this takeover was greeted with extreme hostility in Lima and was followed by rioting in which, according to *Latin America*, 'more than 500 arrests were made, mainly in the middle-class suburbs of Miraflores and San Isidro.'[5] Nevertheless, the government's complete press monopoly was

[4] See *Latin America*, 16 March 1976.
[5] 9 August 1974. These riots also owed something to the presence of Raúl Castro and a number of recently-purchased Russian tanks on the Peruvian military parade of 28 July. These new tanks were intended to impress the Chileans, but had most effect upon the Lima middle class. Like the Duke of Wellington, the Peruvian middle class appears to have said 'We do not know what effect these troops will have on the enemy but by God they terrify us'.

temporarily established later that year, with the closure in November of the independent weeklies, *Oiga* and the *Peruvian Times*. The government's problems with the press, however, were still only beginning.

Possibly in order to try to conciliate the newspaper readership, but also no doubt because of the radicals' participationist ideology, the regime indicated that the press was to be given considerable freedom now that the generally oligarchic economic interests, which had previously controlled it, had been dispossessed. Indeed, certain newspapers took an extremely vigorous line against what they saw as abuses by members of the government, so much so, in fact, that the military hardliners soon added press 'insubordination' to their growing list of grievances about the course of events. Thus, in September 1974, *Nueva Cronica* unleashed a campaign against torture, to which Velasco responded by sacking the head of the police force responsible and charging a number of other police officers with crimes. A month later, the same newspaper broke the story of a corruption network in the food marketing concern Epsa. This led to the arrest of over 100 employees, and the resignation of Luis Barandiarán, a noted military conservative, who was Minister of Trade.[6]

[6] The EPSA case was subsequently taken up by *Oiga* (25 and 31 October 1974), which accused the government of a cover-up and called for the resignation of the Agriculture Minister, General Váldez Angulo. *Oiga* and the *Peruvian Times* also carried stories relating to the attack on a government contract with Japan for a loan to build the trans-Andean pipeline which was made by the Lima Bar Association (a Right-wing association) on nationalistic grounds. These stories, and references made by both magazines to government secrecy about the growing foreign debt, led to their closure in November 1974.

However, the press certainly did not cover everything. Thus, in mid-1975, the Peruvian Air Force staged a public demonstration of the fire power of their new French Mirages (whose purchase had seriously complicated Peruvian–American relations in 1968) and attracted a large crowd to the Chorrillos beaches. The spectacle, however, did not go off quite as planned. The Mirages had a number of fishing boats as targets but, to the increasing delight of the crowd, proved quite incapable of sinking them. Finally, after half an hour of frustration, one pilot became desperate and flew low over the boats, missing them and plunging into the sea. The demonstration was then abandoned with the fishing boats leading by one sinking to nil. Not a word of this story appeared in the Peruvian press, and one foreign correspondent who mentioned the incident was promptly deported. See *Latin American Times*, 21 and 24 July, 1975.

In fact, General Segura, who was directly in charge of the nationalized press, was a notorious hard-liner. Thorndike provides a fascinating account of this period in his *No! Mi General*.

Social Property

The press nationalization was not the only initiative taken by the radicals. Social property legislation, which had been under discussion ever since the military coup, took a major place on the political agenda in August 1973 with the publication of a draft law. This timing clearly had much to do with technical and bureaucratic factors, but a decision to speed up internal deliberations was clearly made by Velasco when, just after his recovery from illness, he chose General Váldez Palacio (another military radical) to head a new commission on the question.[7] Once the draft law was issued, the debate quickly gathered force. The Right argued that social property was a contradiction in terms and thus either an expensive nonsense or a backdoor means of establishing government control.[8] Its more moderate members contented themselves with pointing out that private property would be endangered if social property companies (which were to be owned by their workforce) were given significant competitive privileges, and that the budget would be strained if they were to be subsidized by the state. APRA also found time to attack the law, both on the grounds that it would hurt small and medium sized business[9] and because it was a Yugoslav import which would not work in Peru.[10] The Left, on the other hand, was keen to ensure that social property companies were given the means to compete effectively with the private sector, and thus enabled to play a substantial role in the economy. After all, if social property could not displace existing companies, it was difficult to see how it could carve out a major economic role.[11]

[7] The social property law is discussed in detail by Peter Knight, 'New Forms of Economic Organisation in Peru; Towards Workers Self-Management', in Lowenthal (ed.), *The Peruvian Experiment*, pp. 350–402.
[8] See for example, the comments of Beltrán, *La Realidad Peruana*, pp. 93–6.
[9] *Oiga*, 24 October 1975.   [10] *Caretas*, 8 May 1975.
[11] Without such conversion, there was little chance that the sector could take on major importance. Thus, according to Knight op. cit., p. 393, 'if the private and co-operative sectors expand at even modest rates, and if there is no significant conversion... the social property sector will not be able to reach "predominance" within fifteen years. Assuming that the private sectors do not stagnate, the choice is more dramatic; either there is fairly massive conversion of existing holdings, or predominance of the new sector within the forseeable future is a pipedream.' Moreover, even the transfer of the existing co-operative sector to social property was opposed by APRA on the grounds that the position of the permanent plantation workers might be damaged.

The eventual law, which was issued in May 1974, was less radical than its Right Wing critics had feared. The radical proposals offered by the ex-Minister of Industry—Dellepiane—were ignored, and several limiting provisions were included in order to reassure the business sector. These included a clause asserting that no transfer of existing companies was contemplated, and terms making such conversion extremely difficult. Nevertheless, not everybody was reassured. Other legislation—such as the land reform—had been extensively modified in the course of its implementation and the same process might again be repeated. Thus, however limited its immediate application, the law was at least potentially important and, had it not been overtaken by events, its long-term impact might well have been considerable. Moreover, this impact could only be felt in one direction. However much its radical implications may have been played down at the time, it was nevertheless another move against the private sector.

The Politics of Labour and the MLR

Mid-1974 was the high water mark for the military radicals. This was marked by the publication, in July 1974, of Plan Inca.[12] This was said to have set out the priorities of the military radicals when they took power in 1968, and it covered a wide ranging series of objectives extending from the nationalization of basic industry and the creation of an efficient planning apparatus to the emancipation of women and the reform of education. In fact, it is doubtful whether this document was wholly drawn up in 1968; it is more likely that large parts of the Plan—at least—were added subsequently. However, the issuing of the Plan in July 1974 was appropriate, since this was the last occasion on which the military radicals appeared in control; in the following two years, the military Right gathered strength until—in July 1976—it was able to assert its ascendancy.

It is difficult to place an exact date on the revival of the Peruvian Right, but one early benchmark was laid by the Chilean military coup of September 1973. Indeed this coup boosted the morale of conservatives throughout the continent—and it apparently helped the new group of military hardliners

[12] This is reproduced in English by the *Peruvian Times*, 2 August 1974.

to crystallize in Peru. There is no doubt that Velasco was worried by events in Chile—as he made clear in his reactions to the Southern riots of November 1973.[13] In fact, it is possible that in the following months the Chilean government intervened directly in Peruvian politics; according to one source, Dina (the Chilean secret police agency) made financial contributions to 'the Peruvian Navy and Press, particularly... *Equis X* and *Opinión Libre*.[14] These journals supported APRA and *Acción Popular* respectively.

More immediately, the Southern rioting, which so bady discredited Sinamos, induced certain Right Wing officers to try to establish their own systems of popular mobilization. One of the most active in this respect was General Tantaleán, who had already, in 1972, founded CTRP. This may have been consciously designed to rival Sinamos and was certainly intended to win support away from the Communist-led (and government supporting) CGTP. Indeed, rivalry between the CTRP and the CGTP led to a series of riots and disputes in Chimbote, which began in the fishmeal sector, and spilled over into the steel industry, where considerable damage was done by sabotage. This conflict was a serious setback for Tantaleán, since it allowed Sinamos to take over the CTRP and promptly to downgrade it.

Undaunted, Tantaleán made a further attempt to build up a labour organization loyal to himself, in the shape of the MLR. This began to make an impression in 1974, and, although deeply resented by the military radicals, it came to play a major part in the politics of the regime. The MLR was basically a strike breaking force, and soon, 'took on the characteristics of an almost paramilitary political group, backing strident

[13] These riots were extremely serious, since they swept all of the major cities of the South (Arequipa, Cuzco, Puno and Ayacucho). The South had always been a stronghold of opposition to the regime, which had, after all, toppled a Southerner from the Presidency. The 1973 riots were initiated by SUTEP, the dissident and Aprista led teachers' union, and were followed up by students, small farmers and other groups. After the riots had been put down, Velasco remarked that 'extremists who believe that what has happened in other countries could happen here are mistaken'. (*Latin America*, 30 November 1973.) There can be no doubt that this reference was to Chile.

[14] This was alleged in *The Guardian*, 5 February 1977, which quoted as evidence a photocopied letter from the head of Dina to Pinochet which was dated 16 September 1975. Its authenticity has been confirmed by interview sources.

anti-Communist rhetoric with direct action'.[15] The MLR could count on the support of the increasingly prominent group of military hardliners within the government. These included General Zavaleta, who had replaced General Leonidas Rodríguez as head of Sinamos in 1973, and General Richter, the Interior Minister, whose unhappiness with Velasco had long been common knowledge. There was also A. F. G. Sala, who had once been regarded as a military radical (and was a close personal friend of Velasco) but who became a notably conservative Labour Minister after the beginning of 1975. As already noted the hard-liner, General Segura, was strategically placed in control of the nationalized press, which was used to provide appropriate 'news' about the labour situation. Finally, the group could count on the backing of most of the navy, including Admiral Jiménez de Lucio who was Industry Minister and, as such, concerned to liberalize the investment climate and achieve a *rapprochement* with the private business sector; Jiménez had earlier been exasperated by attacks made on him by the *Comunidades*. The MLR also sought support from Velasco and the radicals with the argument that, with the failure of Sinamos, manipulation was the only alternative to open class conflict. Given the basic authoritarianism of the army, this argument was often persuasive.

Above all, however, the MLR provided a means of connecting APRA with the regime. Ever since 1968, APRA had offered to support the government in return for what it hoped would be concessions and an opportunity to undermine the regime from within. Consequently, it sought to strengthen its position by infiltrating the bureaucracy,[16] and seeking the support of friendly army officers such as Tantaleán, who was related to APRA by marriage and whose son was an active member of APRA's youth movement. APRA saw support for the MLR as a way of splitting the army, and its 'anti-Communism', apart from expressing an old political animosity, was intended to set military hardliners against one of the regime's few sources of civilian support. Indeed, with the nationalists now on the defensive, the way was open for a return to the 'anti-Communist' values which had once been so influential.

[15] *Latin America*, 21 March 1974. See also Thorndike, op. cit.
[16] *Marka*, 7 May 1975.

The MLR's most vocal opponents were to be found among the journalists newly appointed to the nationalized press. These were by no means uniform in their outlook; indeed, one of the newly-appointed editors, Ismael Frias, campaigned against Communist infiltration of the regime and seemed eager to promote a *rapprochement* between APRA and the military hardliners. Most of the other editors, however, identified themselves with the Left and regarded the growing influence of the hardline faction with dismay. Indeed, the press and the MLR came close to open confrontation in a dispute over Marcona in early 1975. This began when the latter tried to destroy the power of the CGTP which, up until then, had enrolled the Marcona ironworkers. The Communist resistance was highlighted in the Lima press. This, apart from giving verbal support to the CGTP, also published the results of an economic study which the latter had commissioned, which claimed that Marcona had been using transfer pricing techniques to avoid paying taxes in Peru, and that it had broken the law over the *Comunidad*. The study thus called for the nationalization of the company without compensation.[17] In doing this, it gave an opportunity to the military radicals to try to regain the initiative by reviving the old nationalist battlecries and dramatics. Thus, in July 1975, Marcona was suddenly expropriated and the regime at first announced that it would not pay compensation. If this was a radical counterattack, however, it failed. Most officers were unimpressed by the takeover (which does not appear to have been discussed in the Council of Ministers) and many were worried that Peru's economic difficulties would now be intensified. The military radicals' initiative had thus served to isolate them further.

APRA and the Peruvian Middle Class

The regime's failure to mobilize effective popular support, and its consequent loss of the 'labour' issue to the hardliners, was made even more serious by the growing hostility of much of the middle class. Up until mid-1974 the regime's willingness to compromise and its determination not to press for seriously

[17] This demand was echoed by the mineworkers' trade union leaders. An interview with one of these—Manuel Orrego—appears in *Marka*, 10 May 1975.

divisive measures had at least secured the apparent political neutrality of the Lima middle class (although this was not true of the provincial areas).[18] Certainly, private investment had fallen off and there were strong conservative pressures on the regime, but commercial interest groups evidently felt it worth their while to continue to negotiate on specific issues (such as the reform of the *Comunidad*) rather than adopting a position of intransigent hostility to the regime as a whole.[19]

However, the press nationalization provided something of a last straw. Not only was this followed by rioting in Lima but also, later in the year, there were several attempts to kill prominent military officers which although unsuccessful increased the political tensions surrounding the regime. APRA was the main beneficiary of this change and it greatly improved its position in Lima in late 1974.[20] Moreover, as we shall see, pressure within this party for a showdown with the military was growing now that the attitude of the middle class had apparently undergone a decisive change.

The Government's Economic Strategy, 1969–74

The military regime faced a further set of problems as a result of the deterioration of the Peruvian economy which began around the middle of 1974 and led to crisis in 1975–6. This

[18] Thus, for example, in 1971 a proposed Educational Reform which would have closed Peru's private schools was rejected in the Council of Ministers (with Montagne reportedly leading the opposition). Moreover, although *Oiga* and certain military radicals had been pressing for a reform of urban land tenure, very little was done. On the 1969–72 period, see D. Collier, op. cit., pp. 116–18. Finally, there was very little in the way of radical tax reform, although tax enforcement improved somewhat under Velasco. Indeed, according to the I.M.F. the 'Tax effort' in Peru actually fell slightly between 1966–8 and 1969–71. See the IMF *Survey*, 3 June 1974. These limitations and compromises led some observers to see the Velasco government as 'middle class', although this view appears very much oversimplified.

[19] Some ministers, such as Admiral Jiménez de Lucio (the Industry Minister after 1971) and A. F. G. Luis Barandiarán (Trade Minister in 1974) appeared particularly receptive to representations from the business community.

[20] There was certainly a world of difference between the somewhat dispirited Aprista rally to celebrate Haya's birthday on 22 February 1974 and the triumphant rally of February 1975, which was the largest Peru had seen since Velasco's illness in 1973. See *Oiga*, 27 February 1975. It is interesting that whereas the rioters of July 1974 chanted slogans in support of *Acción Popular*, their counterparts in February 1975 showed themselves to be pro-Aprista. It is possible that Belaúnde, himself (unlike Haya) in exile, did not have the organization necessary to turn sympathy into active support. This apparent failure was the subject of some comment in Lima at the time.

crisis can only be understood fully after a brief discussion of the course of the Peruvian economy since 1968. We have already seen that the economy was, in 1968, heavily export-dependent and (at least in the modern sector) substantially foreign-owned. Since the military radicals came to power in large part as a reaction against foreign ownership, and since their political base within the military as a whole was always precarious, the government as a whole needed to take on the difficult task of transforming the economy while continuing to depend upon a reasonable degree of conventional economic success. If the economic transformation proceeded too slowly, the radicals would object (and, since they were well-established in the economic ministries, they were well placed to make their opinions heard) but if consumption were squeezed too strongly, the resulting discontent would be likely to permeate the military as a whole.

Within these constraints, the government's economic policies appeared for a time to be successful. The basic aim was to buy room for manoeuvre by signing a number of contracts with foreign companies for very large projects in the belief that it would be possible to borrow against the export income that was expected to result. This borrowing and future tax revenue could then be used to transform the economy without squeezing existing middle class groups. Thus, at the end of 1969, the government signed a contract with the Southern Peru Copper Company for the development of the massive copper deposits at Cuajone.[21] After this contract was signed, the Mines Minister Fernández Maldonado, was given a free hand to develop the rest of the mineral sector and used it to assume direct state control over all other unexploited mineral deposits through the state company—Mineroperú. In somewhat similar fashion, direct foreign investment was allowed into the oil exploration venture that was taking place in Amazonia, while the state company—Petroperú—not only participated in the same venture, but also took exclusive control of refining, marketing and petrochemicals.[22]

[21] The negotiations leading up to this contract are well described by Hunt in 'Direct Foreign Investment in Peru; New Rules for an Old Game' (pp. 326–31) in Lowenthal (ed.), op. cit., pp. 302–49. See also *Oiga*, 7 and 14 November 1969.
[22] See author's D.Phil., to which reference has already been made.

This strategy inevitably imposed tremendous responsibilities upon the state sector and these became even more pronounced as it became apparent that the regime had unintentionally discouraged much domestic as well as foreign private investment. Even when foreign technology was bought with foreign loans, the state companies still had responsibilities of coordination and overall control. Moreover, the regime's sharp change in economic emphasis was necessarily accompanied by the creation of a considerable number of entirely new state companies which needed time to build up viable organizations before undertaking ambitious investment projects. Inevitably, therefore, there were failures. By no means all of the state organizations were inefficient, and several well-placed observers considered that the overall performance of the public sector was good.[23] Nevertheless, in many cases, the burden was too great. Some organizations simply failed to take off and there were many others which, while probably carrying out sound long-term investments, swallowed up large amounts of capital and took far longer to produce results than had been hoped. Thus, the Cerro Verde copper mine, which had been wrested from the control of Anaconda during 1970 and was considered to be easily the most commercial of all of Mineroperú's properties, was initially planned to go onstream in 1974, but did not do so until 1977. Similarly, the Amazonian oil boom had, in 1972, been expected to generate huge sums from the middle of the decade. As it turned out, however, this venture, which attracted both public and private capital in massive quantities did not live up to early hopes even though it was largely rescued by the oil price rises of 1973-4. Thus, in mid-1976 it was expected that large-scale oil production would not begin until 1978 and that Peru would earn no more than a modest surplus after repayments of debt and interest.[24]

For a time, foreign loan capital was so abundant that borrowing appeared to pose no problem at all. Indeed, in 1973-4 it became so easy as to raise money abroad that the Planning Institute was deliberately trying to maximize the foreign exchange cost of projects on the ground that capital was easier

---

[23] This judgement is made, for example, by Fitzgerald, op. cit., pp. 53-4.
[24] *Andean Report*, April 1976.

THE CRISIS 1973-76 149

to raise internationally than domestically.[25] However, as the balance of payments deficit grew, Peru became more and more dependent upon loans and its foreign debt position became less and less satisfactory. Consequently, the world recession of 1974-6 and the subsequent reduction in Peru's creditworthiness,

Table 3: Peru's Balance of Payments 1970-5 (*in* US $m.)

	1970	1971	1972	1973	1974	1975
Exports	1034.3	892.7	942.8	1041.1	1505.3	1378
of which Fish products	338.0	336.1	278.8	148.7	241.9	n.a.
Imports (cif)	−699.6	−751.7	−796.7	−1018.5	−1908	−2491
Service and transfers	−149.8	−193.3	−164.7	−252.4	−322	−455
Current Balance	+184.9	−33.9	−31.7	−173.6	−724.9	−1568
Long Term Capital	23.7	−28.2	115.0	354.6	745.2	1137
of which official	100.5	14.5	116.6	282.3	619.5	n.a.
Errors, Omissions and short run capital	48.8	−14.1	−32.9	−167.8	261.6	−112
Balancing item*	−257.4	76.2	−50.4	−13.2	−281.9	+543

*Minus = inflow   *Source:* B.C.R *Memoria* annual.

[25] Personal communication. Looking back on this period, the *Andean Report* commented that 'between 1971 and 1973 there tended to be more money available than there were properly prepared projects to spend it on', with the consequence that 'big ministry buildings were especially in vogue despite the specific overall planning instructions to the contrary'. February 1976.

However, already by 1974, the Peruvian government was showing signs of anxiety about its foreign exchange position, especially when the price of copper began to fall around the middle of the year. Thus in May, the government began to ration foreign exchange but did so extremely abruptly and thus caused an outcry from the private sector which resulted in the resignation of the Minister of Finance (allegedly on health grounds) in July. Later in the year, the *Peruvian Times* complained that observers 'have become increasingly worried in the past few years by the unavailability of the regular flow of economic information and straighforward statistics which used to be available'. (8 November 1974.) In the week after this appeared, the *Peruvian Times* was closed by the government.

came as a very sharp blow. Already, in 1972, Peruvian exports had been badly hurt by the collapse of the fishmeal industry as a result of unforeseen climatic changes. Fishing was resumed in 1974, but the catch was carefully restricted to well below its previous levels. Overall, therefore, Peru's trade deficit mounted very sharply indeed after 1973, and, after around the middle of 1975, this could no longer be balanced against long term capital inflows. Once this happened, austerity could no longer be postponed.

Austerity measures, however, never popular at the best of times, had now become almost impossible to impose without a major change in the government's political outlook. This in turn required that the succession crisis be settled quickly. It had been different in 1968-9, when the military government could claim to have been clearing up after the excesses of the Belaúnde regime, but after six years in power and after the making of so many promises the military could not impose austerity measures without a sense of failure. Scapegoats might now be needed, and foreign capitalists, whose support was now necessary if drastic spending cutbacks were to be avoided, were not available for such a role.

The military radicals might provide an easier target. Certainly, the takeover of Marcona, so far from rekindling the nationalist beacon, went a long way towards convincing many officers that the radicals needed to be kept in check. Moreover, the obvious facts that austerity measures would be unpopular, and would need to be accompanied by labour repression if they were to succeed, created further problems for the military radicals and their ideology of participation; the popular organizations were permitted to applaud the government's performance, but they were not expected to criticize. If applause was unlikely under the circumstances, the military hardliners would be only too pleased to impose silence.

Military Politics

There were, therefore, a number of reasons why military unity in general, and the radical-developmentalist coalition in particular, were likely to come under strain. Conflicts over labour politics and press ownership, inability to make a clear choice between support for private investment or social property, and growing unease about the state of the economy were compounded by the political uncertainty created by Velasco's illness. However, while some of these differences led to the creation of clear-cut factions within the officer corps, this was not always true. Indeed, the political alignments that were formed during the immediate battle for the succession were somewhat confused and provided a poor guide to the underlying trends within the military. These only became fully clear after Morales had succeeded to the Presidency in August 1975.

After the failure of Mercado's attempt to replace Velasco in March 1973, Morales Bermúdez came to be regarded as Velasco's heir apparent. Morales was acceptable to the military radicals while at the same time being sufficiently conservative to win widespread support from the rest of the officer corps.[26] Since he was not due to retire until 1978, he could simply be made the natural successor to Mercado after the latter's scheduled retirement at the beginning of 1975. Accordingly, in November 1973 it was announced that Morales would become military Chief of Staff during 1974, and would then become Prime Minister in the following year.

Upon hearing of Morales' appointment, Mercado is said to have replied that 'a lot can happen in a year'. Nevertheless, he proved unable to obstruct the President's plans, and Morales, who had won widespread respect from many sides for his skill as Finance Minister, was able to hold together the coalition of 1968 for a little longer. There was, however, one major change. Under Velasco, the radicals always had the ear, and often the active support, of the President. Morales himself, however, was no radical—he was merely more acceptable to the radicals than any other probable candidate, and the most likely to draw conservative support away from Mercado. Thus, in any government that he might form the political tone would almost certainly become more conservative. The radicals must have been aware of this, but felt that in the climate of the day Morales offered the prospect of at least a certain basic continuity with

---

[26] According to a report in the *Washington Post* 'a group of colonels and generals met privately with Velasco [in 1974] and exacted a promise that General Morales will be formally recognised as his successor', 25 January 1975.

the Velasco regime and that they could not expect more. When even this prospect failed them it was already too late.

Thus, Morales was a compromise. He was elevated to the Prime Ministership as an alternative to Mercado, and he later reached the Presidency as an alternative to Tantaleán. Tantaleán, like Mercado, was a hard-liner and his rapid rise to prominence, as well as being a consequence of the latter's decline, was a sign of the growing importance of the hardliners within the military. These, with their emphasis on order and discipline, stood in sharp and deliberate contrast to the radicals' emphasis on participation and popular involvement. Their short-term strength was greatly increased by Tantaleán's close personal association with Velasco which can be explained in terms of their common family links with the Aprista party.[27] Indeed, when after March 1975 Velasco's deterioration in health became very rapid, his Aprista wife became increasingly influential as the guardian of access to him. Consequently, Velasco came to be surrounded by an 'inner circle' which included several Apristas and the most prominent military hardliners. These included Richter, Sala, Jiménez de Lucio and Zavaleta as well as Tantaleán himself. These had all been friends of Velasco and now, with the latter ailing, were eager to extract the maximum benefit from the offices which they now held. Consequently, there came to be a marked increase in corruption. Perhaps the most notorious case of this was provided by Velasco's brother-in-law Gonzalez Posada, who was on the payroll of eight different public enterprises at the same time.[28] Military officers were also involved, however. Indeed corruption in the fishing industry was so notorious that Tantaleán was actually arrested for a time after Morales' coup.[29]

[27] It certainly appears that, despite his earlier radicalism, Velasco was moving closer to the position of the hardliners, particularly after his illness in March 1975. He was certainly close to Tantaleán personally, perhaps because of common family connections with APRA. However, the importance of personalities can be exaggerated, as is clear from the fact that a number of other former radicals switched to the hard-liners during 1975.

[28] See the article by Bermejo in *Nueva*, January 1976.

[29] Bermejo, ibid., quotes Malplica as saying that 'Tantaleán managed Pescaperú as if it were his private property. One day, when the idea occurred to him, he gave 20m. soles to a football club'.

Moreover, it was becoming increasingly clear during 1975 that the group had designs on power as well as income. It faced opposition, therefore, not only from the military radicals, but also from much of the rest of the officer corps. These may not have had strong political commitments, but they appear to have been angered by the growth of open corruption, suspicious of the motives of Tantaleán's supporters, and worried by the continued support which they gave to the MLR (and thus, indirectly, to APRA). Consequently, it was no problem for Morales to win the support of officers who were directly in command of troops, and, in the early part of 1975, he toured all of the military regions of Peru in a successful bid for personal support. Consequently, when he became ready to launch a coup, which he did on 29 August, he knew that he could rely on all five army commands. His coup was followed by the dissolution of the MLR, and by the removal of the more notorious hardliners. Several military radicals were initially given cabinet positions, and, in a promise of continuity with the 'revolution', Fernández Maldonado was promoted to army chief of staff with the intention that he should take over as Prime Minister at the beginning of 1976.

The End of the 'Revolution'

Even though Morales may have wished to maintain continuity with Velasco, however, circumstances made it impossible for him to do so. The coup did no more than clear the air for a time: the underlying political problems, which were now severe, remained unresolved.[30] Consequently, while much is still unclear about Morales' regime, it is evident that the military radicals were decisively defeated during his first year. During this time, there were several political upheavals which often involved resignations from the government. The most prominent departures were, first Graham, the ex-head of Coap, who was no ally of Morales and who did not appear in his cabinet; subsequently Leonidas Rodríguez, who resigned in

---

[30] *Marka* (25 September 1975) perceptively remarked that while the supporsers of the Morales coup were a heterogeneous group, 'one feels that the progressive-radical tendency does not have enough strength to play a decisive part in the political orientation of the regime'.

November 1975 after a conflict about promotions,[31] and finally Fernández Maldonado, Gallegos, and de la Flor who resigned together in July 1976. All appear to have gone quietly, however, convinced that the future of military radicalism was, for the time being at least, hopeless. The reasons for this judgement can be understood clearly enough after an outline of the political forces at work during 1975 and early 1976.

By far the most important feature in the political transformation was the deteriorating state of the economy. There had already, in June 1975, been a series of economic measures aimed at reducing the budget deficit and increasing food output; food prices went up sharply, as did gasoline prices, as a result of the reduction in government subsidies and the payment of higher prices to producers. For a time, it seemed possible that these measures would be sufficient. Indeed, the *Andean Report*, which was extremely unfriendly to the military radicals, still remarked that,

this year's outlook may well seem unhappy. But it is still well short of tragedy; and doomwatch predictions should be treated with extra care... The key considerations seem to be that it is accepted in international banking circles that Peru is a fair risk and the members of the World Bank's Paris Club, at the meeting in March, confirmed that they were prepared to back a lot of specific new projects.[32]

During the rest of the year, however, the world recession continued, and this, together with the problems posed by the Marcona seizure, led to a massive drain on Peru's currency

[31] According to information provided by *Oiga* and *Latin America*, the resignation of Leonidas Rodríguez appears to have been related to an upheaval in the air force which had its roots in the near-naval revolt of early 1975. According to *Oiga* (24 October 1975), the navy, in April 1975, demanded the removal of the pro-regime Admiral Faura and were all set to stage an open rebellion. A. F. G. Gilardi called for the forceful suppression of the navy, and this left him in open conflict with the majority of the air force as well as much of the army. Consequently, once Velasco had been removed, the air force conservatives were able to force the removal of Gilardi. Velasco's influence was not yet extinct, however, and he was still able (according to *Latin America*, 24 October 1975, and 2 January 1976) to induce a majority of air force officers to demand the removal of Gilardi's opponents (Podestá Jiménez, Fernando Miró Quesada Bahamonde and Cesar Yepez) from the government and the promotion to Air Force Minister of Dante Poggi, who had been an ally of Tantaleán and Richter. In order to prevent a similar development in the Lima Armoured Division, Morales purged several officers without consulting Leonidas Rodríguez who was its commander and who, furious at such interference, promptly resigned.

[32] July 1975.

reserves. These fell from US$693m. at the end of 1974 to US$150m. at the end of 1975. Thus, in January 1976, a further deflationary package was announced—gasoline prices were raised again, and taxes were also increased on income and on purchases of foreign currency. Subsequently, in February, Peru began discussions with the World Bank and the IMF. Two months later, it formally opened debt refinancing negotiations with a consortium of foreign banks. It soon became clear that existing measures were no longer enough, and that the public sector would not escape the cuts. Thus, in June, a further austerity package was imposed, including, for the first time, a cut in government spending, as well as a devaluation of the Sol by 31 per cent. These measures were immediately followed by a period of unrest within the army, which culminated with the resignation of Fernández Maldonado at the end of July.[33] Eight days after this resignation it was announced that the government had come to a provisional agreement with a group of New York banks for a loan of $240m. which was to be made conditional on these banks being given extensive, and unprecedented, powers to monitor the progress of the Peruvian economy for the next two years.[34]

[33] It is significant that Fernández Maldonado was forced out despite his expressed willingness to accept, and even introduce, the austerity measures of June 1975. Indeed, ever since Morales' coup, Peruvian conservatives singled out Fernández Maldonado for bitter attack; *Opinión Libre*, for example, as early as 4 December 1975, went so far as to say that 'the presence of General Fernández Maldonado as Prime Minister is more than worrying', which brought it a sharp rebuke from Morales. However, by 12 July 1976, the navy felt sufficiently confident to demand Fernández Maldonado's head on a platter, and this time it was successful (see *Latin America*, 30 July 1976).

[34] This last request is generally regarded as having given the *coup de grâce* to the military radicals. Thus, according to the *New York Times* (4 August 1976) 'the Peruvian government, in power since 1968 as a revolutionary government appears to be coming apart. The government is under pressure from a consortium of United States private banks that are making strict economic and political demands in exchange for loans to cope with huge foreign debts. As the fortunes of the leftist military regime have declined, its dependence on Western financial institutions has become increasingly clear.' From the imperfect information which we have, this interpretation appears justified. It is interesting that Peru began negotiations with the American bankers on 11 July (see the interview in the October 1976 issue of *International Investor* with Carlos Santistevan, the head of the Banco Central de Reserva) and on 12 July the navy reportedly demanded Fernández Maldonado's resignation by the end of that month. It has also been reported (*Latin America*, 30 July 1976) that the Planning Institute, which provided much of the intellectual backing for the military radicals, was excluded from the crucial meeting of the Peruvian Cabinet and, subsequently, purged.

This darkening economic climate made the regime even more vulnerable to popular protests. The Left was able to organize a certain amount of disruption, particularly in the countryside, but by far the most formidable opposition was now provided by APRA. Thus, in February 1975, Lima was shaken by a riot which amounted to a semi-insurrection. This was Aprista-organized (a fact openly admitted by Haya himself). It began with a police strike and was followed up by demonstrating and looting which was evidently well-organized. APRA justified this move in terms of its opposition to 'Communism' and to the social property legislation, but it is possible that its real objective was to destroy the position of the military radicals. Certainly, by February 1975, APRA could count on the support of much of the army, almost the whole navy and the vast majority of the Lima middle class (some of whom may have been pressing for some kind of dramatic action).[35] It is also possible that APRA was supported by the American government.[36] Moreover, the occasion for the riot (a strike by the police, who demanded better pay and conditions) demonstrated the extent to which APRA had penetrated the security forces. Thus, while the riot was suppressed, it undoubtedly inflicted a severe shock upon the regime,[37] which—feeling un-

[35] According to *Caretas* (6 March 1975), Armando Villanueva of APRA met General Vargas Prieto (the army commander-in-chief) and informed him that the impetus to the rioting had come from hot-headed and youthful recruits. While this explanation was convenient, it may have contained some truth.

[36] After the publication of Philip Agee's *CIA Diary* in December 1974, there were many sources only too eager to blame any domestic trouble on the CIA. However, even if one discounts the more alarmist reports, there can be no doubt that the American State Department has traditionally supported APRA (as we have seen in chapter 2) and it is probable that this support intensified as the military government moved further to the Left, and as confrontation with Chile appeared more likely. Moreover, as Peru's financial position worsened, so American diplomatic pressures are likely to have become more persuasive.

There is, in any case, no doubt that APRA could count on the support of the Venezuelan government after the election of President Pérez (of *Acción Democratica*) in 1973. In late 1974, Pérez visited Peru, ostensibly to take part in the Ayacucho celebrations (marking the 150th anniversary of the famous battle) but he nevertheless found time to meet leading Apristas and to recommend the virtues of democracy. See *Caretas*, 20 December 1974. By this time, Venezuela was already a significant lender to Peru.

[37] The *Washington Post* (in my view correctly) attributed the government's delay in putting down the riots not, as was widely believed at the time, to a split within the regime, but to 'sheer disbelief that things had gotten so out of hand'. 24 March 1976.

able to confront APRA—began to look for some kind of accommodation.[38]

The February riots demonstrated more clearly than ever the weakness of popular support for the regime. If austerity measures had become necessary, some deal now had to be struck with APRA if the regime was to avoid total isolation.[39] This was still true after the coup of August 1975 which, while it did remove certain officers who were closely linked with APRA, did not lessen the need for Aprista support. Indeed, Morales' government soon found that it needed Apra even more than its predecessors had. Thus, as austerity measures tightened, the government came under increasing pressure from the hard-line faction to impose 'labour discipline'. Support for such 'discipline' came from within the government itself—from the navy, from several army officers and, after November 1975, from the air force (which controlled the Labour Ministry).[40] Many of these officers were themselves close to APRA.

It is not surprising, therefore, that in May 1976 Morales made a speech at Trujillo in which he called for an end to the historic rivalry between APRA and the military—a gesture which bitterly angered Fernández Maldonado and the other military radicals.[41] APRA reciprocated two months later, when it agreed to use its influence to end a strike of bus drivers in Lima.

With the growing rapprochement with APRA, and the government's increasing need to impose unpopular economic measures, the military regime's own popular organizations came to appear increasingly obsolete. Furthermore, since some of these appeared capable of providing a focal point of opposition to the regime, they needed to be kept under firm control and, where possible, dissolved. Thus, the social property sector, which had never taken a firm hold on the Peruvian economy, was sharply

---

[38] *Caretas*, on March 6 1975, evocatively headlined its edition 'Haya, between war and peace'.

[39] The Communist Party, despite its loyalty, was not nearly strong enough to provide the government with the support which it needed. See *Caretas*, 6 March 1975.

[40] See footnote 31 above.

[41] Indeed, on July 7, 1976, Fernández Maldonado disobeyed orders and commemorated the Trujillo rising, as did a number of younger captains and majors. See *Latin America*, 30 July 1976.

rundown and allowed to go bankrupt.[42] Moreover, the press, which had proved such a valuable ally to the military radicals in 1975, was comprehensively purged in March 1976, when Velasco's appointees were replaced by non-political administrators only too happy to evade any controversial issue.[43] The *Comunidad* concept was also diluted in February 1976, when a decree exempted 'small' companies (generously defined as those with a gross income of under US $0.5m. p.a.) from the need to share power with their workers, although profit sharing would remain.[44]

Thus, by the middle of 1976, the emphasis of the regime had changed almost completely. It had come to rely upon international finance abroad, and on APRA at home, and had begun to dismantle the 'participationist' elements of the Velasco regime in an attempt to encourage private businessmen. It is difficult to say how far the reaction against Velasco's policies will go, or how far the unity of the military will survive such abrupt changes in policy. Nevertheless, it is perhaps possible to suggest why the military radicals proved unable to achieve the hoped-for transformation of Peruvian society.

Essentially, they fell victim to the Velasco regime's inability to choose between very different approaches, and its consequent tendency to end up by pleasing nobody. Thus, popular expectations were first aroused, then manipulated ineffectively, and finally suppressed brutally. The business sector was first alarmed, and then hesitantly courted. The public sector was expanded, but without the imposition of austerity elsewhere, with the result that the regime incurred large debts and continued to borrow until the rate of borrowing became unsustainable. When this happened, it found itself in a renewed, and

[42] According to the *Latin American Economic Review*, 7 January 1977, the government was planning to cut off funds to the sector, cutting the number of enterprises 'in formation' from 63 to 23. One reason for this decision was apparently that the sector was providing another political platform for the radical Left, as became apparent after a meeting of social property workers in Puno in 1976.

[43] In October 1976, for example, Velasco telephoned UPI and complained that he was being kept under house arrest, but not a word of this conversation appeared in any of the Lima dailies.

[44] In a speech to CADE in November 1976, Morales announced that there would be further changes in this law, limiting the share-holding of the *Comunidad Industrial* to a maximum of 33 per cent. See *Latin American Economic Review*, 3 December 1976.

even intensified, state of financial dependency which moved it sharply to the Right. Indeed, it is interesting that, whereas in 1969 the military radicals achieved prominence by attacking economic dependency, in 1976 they fell from power as a result of the dependency which their policies had aggravated.

VII

CONCLUSIONS: THE RISE AND FALL OF THE PERUVIAN MILITARY RADICALS

As we have seen, the rise of a radical military government in Peru posed severe problems for the conventional paradigms through which Latin American politics have been explored. It is not surprising, therefore, that the fall of the radicals tended to confirm observers in their pre-existing views. *Monthly Review* summed up the Peruvian experiment thus:

> the relationships and constraints resulting from the long history of imperialist exploitation are extremely deep rooted. The various reforms aimed at getting out of the dependent relationship ... do not enable the country to overcome the main obstacles. For without the abolition of class exploitation and an accompanying maximum mobilisation of human and natural resources, the potentials for significant self-development are not realisable.[1]

The *New York Times*' analysis was similar: 'as the fortunes of the leftist military regime have declined, its dependence on Western financial institutions has become increasingly clear'.[2]

As always, however, reality is not so clear cut. For one thing, despite their eventual defeat, the military radicals, and their developmentalist allies, made a number of major changes in the Peruvian economy, which appear most unlikely to be reversed. Despite the difficulties with agrarian reform, the regime succeeded in destroying the oligarchy and, in doing so, carried out a measure which was almost certainly necessary, even though not sufficient, if further progress was to be made in the agrarian sector. An entrenched, but hated, oligarchy would increasingly have distracted attention from the real problems of the countryside and might have encouraged populist politicians to discriminate against agriculture in the name of social progress (as happened in Peronist Argentina). Once agrarian reform had

[1] *Monthly Review*, September 1976, p. 21.
[2] *New York Times*, 4 August 1976.

been decreed, even from excessively optimistic expectations, the ensuing problems were likely to force any regime to devote increasing attention—and probably growing resources—to the hitherto—neglected countryside.[3]

Moreover, the creation of a large state sector (which may now be trimmed, but which will probably be left substantially intact) was another step of fundamental importance. For one thing, in Peru continued economic growth tends to require the carrying out of projects on a very large scale in such key sectors as irrigation, mining and petroleum; here detailed 'micro level' information may be essential to effective policymaking. Such information can be reliably acquired only through a large measure of public ownership.[4] Moreover, in a country where no 'national bourgeoisie' has been conspicuous, public ownership may be the only means by which the entrepreneurial energies of the native population can be encouraged. As Hunt pointed out,

having constructed a network of state enterprises destined to control the commanding heights of the economy, Peruvians will become obliged to manage, to administer, and to perform entrepreneurial functions as never before. The benefits to be obtained from successfully meeting this challenge are the greatest of all. It involves nothing less than changing a nation's character in a way that can bring development out of underdevelopment.[5]

---

[3] A. Hirschman has outlined a similar pattern of reform, according to which the initial legislation stems from unrealistic expectations, but the ensuing problems then force the government to tackle the problem (and also related ones) with greater thoroughness and depth. In the case under discussion, it can be seen that the regime's initial decision to destroy the oligarchy eventually led it to tackle the further problem of agrarian production. See A. Hirschman, *Journeys Towards Progress* (New York, 1965).

[4] Several writers have argued that a 'bargaining model' is an effective substitute for direct ownership, in that it enables the state to take a large share of the profits from such large-scale ventures while retaining the benefits of private ownership. However, a number of recent case studies have suggested that, in the absence of a large state sector, such an arrangement has rarely worked well in Spanish America. See A. Pinelo, op. cit.; T. H. Moran, *Multinational Corporations and the Politics of Dependence: Copper in Chile* (Princeton, 1974); and F. Tugwell, *The Politics of Oil in Venezuela* (Stanford, 1975). The problems of applying a bargaining model to the IPC case were also discussed in G. Philip, 'The Limitations of Bargaining Theory: A case study of the International Petroleum Company in Peru', in *World Development*, March 1976.

[5] Hunt, 'New Rules for an Old Game', in Lowenthal (ed.), *Continuity and Change*, p. 347.

There is, of course, always the risk that the state sector will fail; that the 'virus of inefficiency' will, for a time, kill off Peru's chances of rapid economic growth. Whatever the outcome, however, the significance of these changes should not be underestimated. Whatever the financial problems which Peru now faces, Velasco's government did manage to transform the structure of ownership within the economy in a way that surprised observers. The full effect of this transformation has yet to be seen.

It must also be remembered that the fall of the military radicals took place when conditions had become quite exceptionally unfavourable. The world-wide combination of increased oil prices, recession in the industrialized world and growing fears among bankers of the consequences of excessive international lending have had dramatic effects in many other developing countries, for example Argentina, Zaire and North Korea. Moreover, in Peru economic setback coincided with the political problems associated with Velasco's illness. Had political uncertainties not combined with the economic crisis, the radicals might have been able to maintain their position in the government for a good deal longer.

These qualifications are important, but it is still true that many obstacles to effective military radicalism had become apparent in Peru well before the financial *coup de grace* of July 1976. The most important of these obstacles appear to have stemmed from the fact that the regime was a military government and, as such, sharply constrained by its political base. These constraints can be seen in three different ways, and, at this point, it will be useful to reconsider the questions raised in the Introduction.

To begin with, it was asked how a radical military government could come to power in Peru in 1968. This question was subsequently tackled with the argument that military radicalism became possible only because of the weakness of the civilian Left. Evidence for this position can be seen, first, in the 'crossing of paths' between the military and APRA. When APRA was on the Left, the military reacted against it by maintaining a sternly conservative posture and by removing radicals from the officer corps on suspicion of Aprista sympathies. Subsequently, as APRA became more conservative, the position of radical military officers became much easier since it was they who could now claim to be upholding the distinctiveness and independence of the officer corps. Moreover, the nature of the political arguments used over the IPC issue strongly suggest that military nationalism was a substitute for neoliberal and 'anti-subversive' values; as the fear of subversion grew less, so nationalism became more attractive to the army. Finally, an inverse correlation between military and civilian radicalism can be seen throughout Latin America. This situation is most clear cut in Brazil, where the military first supported Vargas, and subsequently intervened against him and his radical successors. In Argentina, Uruguay and Chile, however, fear of chaos and revolution has also recently led to the intervention of military hard-liners, determined to stamp out 'subversion' and encourage capitalism. However, in Ecuador, where a watered down 'Peruvian model' has been tried, the weakness of the civilian Left has been notable. Thus, it appears that the military may occasionally be tempted to move into a vacuum on the Left, but it will see no great attraction in trying to outbid the Marxists in radicalism.[6]

If it is true, however, that the Peruvian military radicals could only come to power as a result of the weakness of the civilian Left, then many of its difficulties can be readily understood. If the electoral Left was weak, then where was the civilian political support which the military sought? If, under conditions of open political competition, there had been an easily organizable class, with a strong commitment to reform, one might have expected some civilian party to have enrolled it. Since no civilian party did so, it was clear that the enrolment of radical supporters might also pose problems for the military.

---

[6] Thus, Huntington argues that 'as society changes, so does the role of the military. In the world of oligarchy, the soldier is a radical; in the middle-class world, he is a participant and arbiter; as a mass society looms on the horizon, he becomes the conservative guardian of the existing order. Thus, paradoxically but understandably, the more backward a society is, the more progressive the role of the military; the more advanced a society becomes, the more conservative and reactionary becomes the role of the military'. *Political Order*, p. 221. Provided that 'advancement' is defined in terms of political mobilization, this appears to be quite accurate, as does S. E. Finer's comment that 'officer corps have been prepared to carry out widespread nationalisation of land and industry, provided they control or lead the mass organisations', S. E. Finer, 'The Mind of the Military', in *New Society*, 7 August 1975, p. 298.

Indeed, as we have seen, military radicalism was not triggered off by any turbulence on the part of groups which had lost out as a result of Peru's pattern of industrialization; rather, it represented an intellectual dissatisfaction with the direction which the Peruvian economy was taking. Left-wing intellectuals alone, however, did not form a particularly impressive power base.

One apparently attractive way for the government to look for popular support was to seek supporters as a result of redistributive measures. It seemed at first as if property could simply be taken from the oligarchy and the more unpopular foreign companies, and used to create a political clientele. The problem was, however, that these 'easy' redistributions did not provide very much income in the short term—certainly not enough to satisfy the expectations aroused by the reforms themselves. The old owners had been given too much warning and had largely decapitalized by the time of their final expropriation. Thus, by 1968, there was not much that could still be squeezed from the *haciendas*, from IPC or from Cerro de Pasco. If redistribution was to be pressed further, however, it would be necessary to move against the smaller domestic companies and against a large section of the labour force. Mere 'populism' would not be sufficient, but it was clear that anything more radical would risk a polarization. If it came to civil war, the military radicals would be ill-equipped.

Indeed, the military radicals could scarcely afford any major confrontation. Historically, Peru has been prone to political violence, and threatened members of the modern sector were always capable (with some help from the opposition political parties) of rioting in defence of what they regarded as their legitimate interests. Yet the military radicals had put forward their reform proposals according to the rationale of counter-insurgency; they had argued that social peace would be increased, not undermined, if sweeping changes took place. However, the rhetoric of counter-insurgency could only encourage reform when there was no real insurgency to counter, and the radicals' position would clearly be weakened if it appeared that reform had the effect of increasing disturbances and social tension. Indeed, if a law-and-order reaction developed, it would become impossible for the military radicals to try to mobilize civilian support and their attempts to redistribute income would then lose their point. Thus, it did not matter that the riots in the South in November 1973, and those in Lima in February 1975, were organized by the Right. Their effect, which was to discredit the radicals in general and Sinamos in particular, was the same as would have resulted from rebellion from the Left.

Moreover, the fact that the military radicals dared not encourage real confrontation ensured that their own agencies for popular mobilization had to be severely circumscribed. 'Supporters' had to be manipulated; they could not be allowed to confront their well-organized conservative opponents. Such manipulation, however, quickly demoralized, or antagonized, those groups which had most hoped to benefit from the government's programme. Thus, one by one, the government's reforms came under attack from those who had been expected to support them and, as these attacks developed, so it appeared that the military radicals had lost control of the situation. Under these circumstances, there were no political advantages for the military in pressing ahead with policies of income redistribution or popular mobilization.

The second question raised in the Introduction concerned the issue of military unity; is the military anything more than an arena within which different political groupings compete for control? If not, then will military disunity undermine any coherent programme, whether reformist or not? As we have seen, it is possible to exaggerate the extent of military disunity. There are always resources in the hands of a military-political leadership and, in Peru, there were good reasons for believing that these would prove to be considerable. An 'institutional' government, a rapidly growing public sector, and a strong tradition of military elitism all made it easier for a military-political leadership to exert control. However, the compromises that were necessary in order to maintain such unity seriously reduced the regime's possibilities of pursuing a coherent strategy, and thus contributed greatly to its failure. Moreover, as with all authoritarian governments, the Peruvian military faced serious problems with the succession. Inevitably, the prolonged illness of the head of state created uncertainty and encouraged open political competition among his would-be successors. In such conditions (as had happened in 1968-9) the views of the officer corps as a whole took on decisive importance and the manipulative abilities of a small military elite ceased to be sufficient to maintain its position. Rather, the preferences of an officer corps which, as a whole, had been frightened by the economic position of the country and disturbed by the failures of the 'popular' institutions pointed to the ascendancy of Morales and the subsequent conservative drift of the regime. Thus, in order to try to reconcile the increasingly influential hard-line 'law-and-order' wing of the military, President Morales was eventually forced to sacrifice the radical officers who had been his colleagues since 1968.

This outcome suggests an answer to the third question raised in the Introduction. Is military radicalism ever viable, or must it eventually fall of its own weight? Evidence from the rest of Latin America has hardly been encouraging for military radicals; neither Vargas nor Perón was able to reconcile leadership of a successful popular movement with the support of the military. These twin horses are notoriously difficult to ride; if the needs of the military are stressed, then the popular movement will provide few rewards and few will be attracted to it. On the other hand, if militant and economically damaging demands are encouraged in order to win popular support, there is likely to be a reaction from the regime's original supporters and, especially, from the military iself.[7]

In Peru, the military radicals lacked the freedom to create effective systems of participation. Velasco himself had no doubt that his primary base of support lay within the military, and whenever this appeared to be threatened by civilian political associations (as with the CDRs in early 1970), he clearly preferred to keep his military supporters even at the risk of antagonizing his civilian allies. Given this decision, it might be argued that the military radicals would have been better advised to abandon their hopes of redistributing power and instead made a more determined effort to implement 'technocratic' advice of a reformist nature. 'Technocratic' reformism might have had

[7] Huntington, ibid., also describes one option open to the military as 'retain and expand', by which he denotes various forms of military populism and attempts at military-led participation. He finds, however, that, such measures tend to intensify divisions within society and also within the officer corps itself. Such a finding is supported by the Peruvian evidence.

sufficient backing from the officer corps for the government to be able to impose the required changes without the need for participation. However, whatever the other disadvantages of such a programme may have been, it simply did not correspond to the objectives of the military radicals in 1969.

While no definite answer is possible, then, the Peruvian case does contribute towards a growing body of evidence which suggests that the problem of participation is the Achilles heel of radical military regimes. Destruction of existing classes may be possible, imposition of change at the point of the bayonet may even be practicable (although the results may not always be those expected) but no regime can indefinitely reconcile open participation with an enforced and unpopular policy.

Nevertheless, the Velasco regime was far from being a total failure. It did carry through a number of major initiatives and was only overthrown after the physical incapacity of the President had become manifest. Under these conditions, it may be rash to generalize too freely from the downfall of the Peruvian military government. After all in 1968 little change was expected from the Peruvian military, and many were later surprised by the direction which it took. There are still enough political options open in Latin America to suggest that there may be further surprises.

BIBLIOGRAPHY

PRIMARY SOURCES

A. Official

Banco Central de Reserva *Memoria 1968–75*
Cuentas Nacionales del Perú 1950–67
Cuentas Nacionales del Perú 1960–73
Cuentas Nacionales del Perú 1960–69

Instituto Nacional de
Planificación *Plan 1971–75.* Pt. 1. *Plan Global*

B. Newspapers and Periodicals

Andean Report
Business Latin America
Caretas
El Comercio
La Cronica (after 1970, *La Nueva Cronica*)
Expreso
Equis X
Financial Times
International Investor
Latin America
Latin American Economic Report
Marka
New York Times
Nueva
Opinión Libre
Oiga
Peruvian Times
La Prensa
Sociedad y Politica
IMF Survey
Survey of Current Business (U.S. Department of Commerce)
Ultima Hora
Washington Post

SECONDARY WORKS

A. Unpublished Private

Ballantine, Janet, 'The Political Economy of the Peruvian *Gran Minería*' (Ph.D., Cornell, 1974).

Bell, W. S., 'The Politics of Agrarian Reform in Peru, 1972–6; the CCP and the CNA' (Mimeo, London, February 1977).

Bertram, I. G., 'Development Problems in an Export Economy; a study of domestic capitalists, foreign firms and government in Peru 1919–30.' (D. Phil.; Oxford, 1974.)

Gilbert, D., 'The Oligarchy and the Old Regime in Peru' (Ph.D., Connell, 1977).

Hunt, S., 'Distribution, Growth and Government Economic Behaviour in Peru' (Woodrow Wilson School, Princeton Univ., 1969).

Lewis, S., 'The IPC in Peru; a case study of nationalism, management and international relations' (Mimeo, Hayward State College, Calif., 1972).

Philip, G., 'Policymaking in the Peruvian Oil Industry, with special reference to the period since 1968' (D.Phil., Oxford, 1975).
Treverton, G., 'Politics and Petroleum; the IPC in Peru' (B.A. Princeton, 1969).
———, 'U.S. foreign policymaking in the IPC case' (Mimeo, Washington D.C., September 1974).
Thorp, R., 'The Expansion of Foreign Ownership in Peru in the 1960's; a perspective on the military's economic policy' (Mimeo, Oxford, 1973).
———, 'The Process of Industrialisation in Peru 1940–1968' (Mimeo, Oxford, 1975).

B. Books and Articles

Agee, P., *Inside the Company; CIA Diary* (London, 1975).
Aguilar Derpich, J., *Perú ¿Socialismo Militar?* (Caracas, 1972).
Astiz, C., *Pressure Groups and Power Elites in Peruvian Politics* (New York, 1969) and, with J. Garcia, 'The Peruvian Military; Achievement, Orientation, Training and Political Tendencies', in *Western Political Quarterly*, November 1972, pp. 667–85.
Bayer, D. L., 'Urban Peru; Political Action as a Sellout', pp. 226–38 of D. Chaplin *Peruvian Nationalism* (New Jersey, 1976).
Beltrán, P., *La Verdadera Realidad Peruana* (Madrid, 1976).
Bergman, A., and Larson, M., *Social Stratification in Peru* (Berkeley, 1969).
Bourricaud, F., *Power and Society in Contemporary Peru* (New York, 1970).
———, (ed.) *La Oligarquía en el Perú* (Lima, 1969).
Chaplin, D. (ed.), *Peruvian Nationalism; A Corporatist Revolution* (New Jersey, 1976).
Clinton, R., 'The Modernising Military; the case of Peru', in *Inter-American Economic Affairs*, vol. 24, no. 4 (Spring 1971), pp. 43–66.
Collier, D., *Squatters and Oligarchs; Authoritarian Rule and Policy Change in Peru* (Baltimore, 1976).
Cotler, J., 'Political Crisis and Military Populism', in *Studies in Comparative International Development*, vol. 6, no. 5 (Spring 1971), pp. 95–113.
———, 'Bases del Corporativismo en el Perú', in *Sociedad y Política*, vol. 2 (October 1972), pp. 3–12.
———, 'Concentración del Ingreso y Autoritarianismo Politico en el Perú', in *Sociedad y Política*, vol. 4 (September 1973), pp. 5–9.
———, 'The New Mode of Political Domination in Peru', in A. Lowenthal, ed., *The Peruvian Experiment*, pp. 44–73.
———, 'The Mechanics of Internal Domination and Social Change in Peru', pp. 35–75 of D. Chaplin, *Peruvian Nationalism*.
Dew, E., *Politics in the Altiplano; the dynamics of change in rural Peru* (Austin, Texas, 1969).
Doughty, P., 'Social Policy and Urban Growth in Lima', pp. 175–222 of D. Chaplin, ed., *Peruvian Nationalism*.
Einaudi, L., 'Revolution from Within? Military Rule in Peru since 1968', pp. 401–27 of D. Chaplin (ed.), *Peruvian Nationalism* and, with A. Stepan, *Latin American Institutional Development; changing perspectives in Peru and Brazil* (Rand Corp., 1971).

Einhorn, J., *Expropriation Politics* (Washington D.C., 1974).
Ferrer, J., 'Peru: The General as Revolutionary', in the *Columbia Journal of World Business*, vol. 5, no. 6 (November–December, 1970).
Finer, S. E., 'The Mind of the Military, in *New Society*, 7 August 1975, pp. 287–9.
Fitzgerald, E. V. K., *The State and Economic Development; Peru since 1968* (Cambridge, 1976).
Gall, N., 'Peru; the Master is Dead', in *Dissent*, 1971, pp. 280–320.
Gallo, E., 'Argentina; Background to the Present Crisis', in the *World Today*, November 1969, pp. 496–504.
Gilbert, A., *Latin American Development; A Geographical Perspective* (London, 1974).
Goodsell, C., *American Corporation and Peruvian Politics* (Cambridge, Mass., 1974).
Goodwin, R., 'Letter from Peru', in the *New Yorker*, 17 May 1969.
Gott, R., *Rural Guerillas in Latin America* (London, 1973).
Grondona, M., 'La izquierda militar en la América Latina; los problemas, las tendencias, y el futuro de la revolución peruana', in A. Canepa Sardon, *La Revolución Peruana* (Buenos Aires, 1971), pp. 35–44.
Handelsman, H., *Struggle in the Andes* (Austin, Texas, 1972).
Harding, G., 'Peru; Questions of Revolution', pp. 185–90, *Latin American Review of Books*, vol. 1 (Spring 1973).
——, *Agrarian Reform and Agrarian Struggle in Peru* (Working Paper no. 15, Centre of Latin American Studies, Cambridge, March 1974).
——, 'Land Reform and Social Conflict in Peru', in Lowenthal, *The Peruvian Experiment*, pp. 220–53.
Hayn, R., 'Peruvian Exchange Controls 1945–8', in *Inter-American Economic Affairs*, vol. 10 (Spring 1957), pp. 47–70.
Hennessy, A., 'Populism in Latin America', in G. Ionescu and E. Gellner, *Populism; its meaning and national characteristics* (London, 1969), pp. 20–61
Hirschman, A., *Journeys Towards Progress* (New York, 1965).
Hunt, S., 'New Rules for an Old Game; Direct Foreign Investment in Peru', in A. Lowenthal (ed.), *The Peruvian Experiment*, pp. 302–49.
Huntington, S. P., *Political Order in Changing Societies* (Yale, 1968).
Kedourie, E., *Nationalism* (London, 1960), and (ed.) *Nationalism in Asia and Africa* (London, 1971).
Klaren, P., *Modernisation, Dislocation and Aprismo; Origins of the Peruvian Aprista Party 1870–1932* (Austin, Texas, 1971).
Knight, P., 'New Forms of Economic Organisation in Peru Towards Workers' Self-Management', pp. 350–402, of Lowenthal (ed.), *The Peruvian Government*.
Levingston, J., and de Onis, J., *The Alliance that Lost its Way* (Chicago, 1970).
Loveday, B. W., *Sanchez Cerro and Peruvian Politics 1930–1* (Occasional Paper, University of Glasgow, 1973).
Lowenthal, A., 'Peru's Ambiguous Revolution' in *Foreign Affairs* July 1974, pp. 799–817, and (ed.) *The Peruvian Experiment: Continuity and Change under Military Rule* (Princeton, 1975).

Malloy, J., 'Authoritarianism, Corporatism and Mobilisation in Peru', *Review of Politics*, vol. 36, no. 1 (Spring 1974), pp. 52-84.
Malplica, C., *Los Dueños del Perú* (3rd ed., Lima, 1968).
March, J., and Simon, H., *Organisations* (New York, 1958).
Marichetti, J., and Marks, A., *The CIA and the Cult of Intelligence* (New York, 1974).
McCoy, N., 'Congress, the President and Political Stability in Peru', pp. 325-69, H. Agor (ed.), *Legislatures in Latin America; their role and influence*.
Miguens, J., 'The New Latin American Military Coup', in *Studies in Comparative International Development*, vol. 1, 1970-1, pp. 3-12.
Miller, R., 'Foreign Firms and the Peruvian Government', in D. C. M. Platt (ed.), *Business Imperialism; an analysis based on the British experience in Latin America before 1930*. (O.U.P., forthcoming).
and ed. (with C. T. Smith and B. Roberts), *Social and Economic Change in Contemporary Peru* (Liverpool, 1976).
Minogue, K., *Nationalism* (London, 1967).
Moran, T. H., *Multinational Corporations and the Politics of Dependence; Copper in Chile* (Princeton, 1974).
Moreira, N., *Modelo Peruano* (Buenos Aires, 1974).
Needler, M., 'Ecuador, 1963', in W. Andrews and V. Ra'anan (eds.), *The Politics of the Coup d'Etat; Five Case Studies* (New York, 1969).
Neustadt, R., *Presidential Power* (New York, 1961).
Niera, H., 'Peru' in J. Bernard et al. *Guide to the Political Parties of South America* (London, 1973), pp. 393-469.
Nun, J., 'The Middle-Class Military Coup', in C. Veliz (ed.), *The Politics of Conformity in Latin America* (Oxford, 1967), pp. 66-118.
Payne, J., *The Peruvian Coup d'Etat of 1962; the Overthrow of Manuel Prado* (Washington D.C., 1968).
Petras, J., and La Porte, R. *Perú; Transformación Revolucionaria o Modernización?* (Lima, 1971).
Philip, G., 'The Soldier as Radical; the Peruvian Military Government 1968-75', in the *Journal of Latin American Studies* May 1976, pp. 29-51.
——, 'The Limitations of Bargaining Theory; a case study of the International Petroleum Company in Peru', in *World Development*, March 1976, pp. 131-239.
Pike, F., *The Modern History of Peru* (New York, 1967).
Pinelo, A., *The Multinational Corporation as a Force in Latin American Politics; A Case Study of the International Petroleum Company in Peru* (NewYork, 1973).
Portocarrero, F., 'La coyontura economica; conciliacion y lucha de clases', in *Sociedad y Politica*, April 1973, pp. 16-19.
Potash, R., *The Army and Politics in Argentina 1928-45* (Stanford, 1969).
Powell, S., 'Political Participation in the Barriadas; A Case Study', in *Comparative Political Studies*, vol. 2 (July 1969), pp. 195-215.
Quijano, A., *Nationalism and Capitalism in Peru* (New York, 1971).
——, 'Conciliación y Lucha de Clases', in *Sociedad y Politica*, vol. 1 (June 1972), pp. 3-12.

Ramirez Novoa, E., *Recuperación de La Brea y Pariñas* (Lima, 1964).
——, *Petróleo y Revolución Nacionalista* (Lima, 1970).
Roberts, B., 'The Social History of a Provincial Town; Huancayo', in R. Miller et al. *Social and Economic Change*, pp. 130–92.
Roemer, M., *Fishing for Growth* (Harvard, 1970).
Roper, C., 'Peru's Long-Standing Problems', in *World Today*, June 1969, pp. 247–54.
Schurmann, A., 'The Communist Party and the State', in A. Pizzorno (ed.), *Political Sociology* (London, 1971), pp. 177–89.
Scott Palmer, D., and Middlebrook, K. *Military Government and Political Development; lessons from Peru* (London, 1975).
Scott Palmer, D., and Susan Bourque, 'Transforming the Rural Sector: Government Policy and Peasant Response', in A. Lowenthal (ed.), *The Peruvian Experiment*, pp. 179–220.
Smith, C. T., 'Agrarian Change and Political Development in Peru', in R. Miller et al., *Social and Economic Change*, pp. 87–119.
Stepan, A. (ed.), *Authoritarian Brazil* (Princeton, 1973).
Sulmont, D., *El Movimento Obrero en el Perú 1900–56* (Lima, 1975).
Thorp, R., and Bertram, G., *Economic History of Peru since 1890* (Cambridge, 1977).
Trias, V., *Fuerzas Armadas y Revolución* (Montevideo, 1971).
Tugwell, F., *The Politics of Oil in Venezuela* (Stanford, 1975).
Utley, T., 'Doing Business with Latin American Nationalists; the case of Peru', *Harvard Business Review*, vol. 5, no. 1 (January–February 1973), pp. 77–86.
Valderrama, M., *7 Años de Reforma Agraria en Perú* (Lima, 1976).
Valdéz Pallete, L., 'Antecedentes de la Nueva Orientación de la Fuerza Armada del Perú', in *Aportes*, no. 19, January 1971, pp. 163–81.
Vargas Haya, *Contrabando* (Lima, 1976).
Villanueva, V., *Un Año Bajo el Sable* (Lima, 1963).
——, *Cien Años del Ejercito Peruano; Frustraciones y Cambios* (Lima, 1971).
——, *El CAEM y La Revolución de la Fuerza Armada* (Lima, 1972).
——, *Ejercito Peruano; del caudillismo anarquico al reformismo militar* (Lima, 1973).
Zimmermann, A., *La Historia Secreta del Petróleo* (Lima, 1968).
——, *El Plan Inca; Objectivo Revolución Peruana* (Lima, 1974).

INDEX

Acción Popular, 5, 38, 45–50, 63, 121; see also Belaúnde
Agee, 64, 156
Agor, 37
Agrarian Reform: 1964, 37, 117–18; 1969, 117–23, 127; see also *La Convención*
Aguilar, Derpich, 89
Air Force, 57, 84, 107, 111, 154, 157
Allende, Salvador, 112
Andean Report, 112, 148, 149, 154
Andrews, 11
Apra, 5, 13, 14, 17–22, 23, 27, 28, 29, 30, 31–5, 38, 39, 40–1, 50, 52, 53, 57, 65, 74, 76, 77, 82, 86, 88, 89, 121, 127, 178, 141, 143, 145, 146, 152, 153, 156–9, 162; see also Haya de la Torre
Arce, Admiral José, 139
Arequipa, 30, 31, 110, 131, 143
Argentina, 123, 162, 163
Arrisueño, General Alfredo, 85, 92, 110
Artola, General Armando, 82, 83, 85, 92, 110, 112, 123
Aspillaga (family), 17, 23, 132
Astiz, 16, 35, 44, 78, 81, 102, 111, 112
Atlas Security Company, 85
Ayachucho, 143
Ayulo (family), 85

Baella, Alonso, 8, 84, 86
Ballantine, 4, 37, 90, 129
Banco de Crédito, 85, 125
Banco Popular, 26–7, 86; see also Prado family
Barandiarán, General Jorge, 95, 101
Barandiarán, General Luis, 101, 140, 146
Barriadas, 27, 28, 29, 103, 130–1

Bayer, David, 50
Bayer Chemical Co, 126
Belaúnde, Fernando (President 1963–1968), 30, 32, 35, 36–8, 43, 44, 45–48, 55, 56, 60, 65, 70, 74, 76, 80, 81, 83, 86, 87, 88, 98, 110, 115, 116, 118, 150; see also *Acción Popular*
Bell, 118, 120, 122, 128
Beltrán, Pedro, 9, 43, 59, 63, 69, 102, 104; see also *La Prensa*
Benavides, Marshal Oscar (President 1933–39), 33, 82
Benavides, General José, 82, 90, 92, 95, 98, 101, 118
Benavides, Alfonso, Correa, 69, 86, 87
Berckemeyer, Fernando, 82, 85
Bertram, 3, 17, 58, 115, 126
Blanco, Hugo, 39, 78
Bourricaud, 15, 26, 29, 63
La Brea, see International Petroleum Company
Briceno, Colonel Gonzalo, 80–1
Business Latin America, 88, 90, 125
Bustamante, Jose Luis (President 1945–48), 13, 16, 31, 33, 36, 71

CAEM, see Centro de Altos Estudios Militares
Camino, Rear-Admiral, 92, 93
Canepa, Sardon, 8
Carbonel, Rear-Admiral, 84, 90, 91
Caretas, 8, 62, 72, 79, 80, 81, 83, 87, 88, 93, 103, 118, 126, 141, 156, 157
Castro, Fidel, 64, 89
Castro, Raúl, 139
Cavero Calixto, General, 85, 87
Centro de Altos Estudios Militares (CAEM), 10, 41–4, 68, 78–9, 83, 85, 102, 105

INDEX

Cerro de Pasco, 15, 18, 23, 24, 82, 118, 128, 132, 164
Cerro Verde, 148
C.G.T.P. (Confederación de Trabajadores Generales del Perú), 143, 145
Chamot, Air Force Major-General Jorge, 84, 92
Chaplin, 3, 25, 49, 50, 135
Chase Manhattan Bank, 27, 86
Chile, 112, 142–3, 156, 163
Chimbote, 131
Chorrillos (military academy at), 76, 79, 126
CIA, 64, 80–1, 132, 156
Civilistas, 17, 33
Club Nacional, 33, 101
Collier, 3, 28, 30, 105, 130, 146
El Comercio, 27, 30, 48, 62, 66, 67, 70, 88, 106, 137, 138, 139; see also Miró Quesada
Comité de Asesores a la Presidencia (Coap), 85, 93, 106, 112, 118, 153
Communist Party of Peru, 22, 38–9, 69, 127, 128–9, 145, 167
Comunidad Industrial, 125–6, 132, 135, 144, 145, 146, 158
Congress, 35–8, 59–60, 65, 69
La Convención, 39, 44, 78
Cornejo Chavez, Hector, 139
Correo, 139
Counter-Insurgency, 41–4, 48, 66, 164; see also Centro de Altos Estudios Militares
Cotler, 4, 6, 49, 94, 119, 126, 129
Cox, Carlos Manuel, 32
La Cronica (including *Nueva Cronica*), 102, 103, 139
C.T.R.P. (Confederacion de Trabajadores de la Revolución Peruana), 143
Cuajone, 71
Cuba, 54, 64, 74, 128
Cuzco, 31, 131, 143

Delgado, Carlos, 6
Dellepiane, Admiral Jorge, 124, 142
Dew, 121

Dianderas, General Roberto, 81
DINA, 143
Dóig Sánchez, General Julio, 46–7, 72, 73, 93
Doughty, 25

Ecuador, 163
Empresa Petrolera Fiscal (EPF), 37, 60, 66, 81, 92
Einaudi, 7, 10, 41, 43, 55, 83, 104, 116, 135
Einhorn, 94
E.P.F., see Empresa Petrolera Fiscal
Espinosa, Fernando, 73
Equis X, 143
Expreso, 30, 84, 87, 89, 92, 103, 138, 139

Faura, Admiral Guillermo, 104, 154
FENCAP, 49
Fernández Maldonado, General Jorge, 78, 85, 87, 92, 93, 114, 119, 123, 136, 147, 152, 154, 155, 157
Ferrand, Ing Jorge, 92
Fenner, 97
Ferrero, Raúl, 85
Financial Times, 87, 94
Finer, 163
Fisher, 4, 19
Fish meal, 23, 24, 25, 28, 30, 149–50
Fitzgerald, 3, 24, 28, 115, 116, 121, 126, 148
Flor, General Miguel de la, 154
Frias, Ismael, 139, 145

Gagliardi, General José, 76, 81
Gall, 77, 79, 83, 84, 103, 112
Gallo, 97
Gallegos, General Enrique, 78, 110–111, 154
García, 78, 111, 112
de Gaulle, Charles, 76
Gervasi, Air Force General Rolando, 84
Gilardi, Air Force General Rolando, 84, 85, 90, 92, 111, 154
Gilbert, Alan, 25
Gilbert, Denis, 15, 17, 25, 76, 85

INDEX

Gildemeister (family), 18, 23
Gonzales Posada, 152
Goodsell, 5, 37, 58, 97
Goodwin, 56, 70, 71, 72, 73
Goulart, Jango, 111
Gott, 39
Grace, W. R., 18, 23, 137
Graham, General José, 85, 153
Grondona, 8
Guevara, Ché, 78
Guardian, The, 143
Gulf Oil, 136

Handelsman, 49, 118, 120
Harding, 78, 119, 120
Haya de la Torre, Victor Raúl, 19, 32, 35, 38, 54, 82, 123, 156; *see also* Apra
Hayn, 16
Heighes, Air Force General José, 84
Hennessy, 20
Herrera Gray, Mario, 86
Hickenlooper Amendment, 67, 94
Hirschman, 161
Hoyos Rubío, General Guillermo, 110, 137
Huancayo, 19, 29
Huanta, 119
Hunt, 24, 37, 64, 92, 147, 161
Huntington, 10, 11, 29, 51, 163, 166

Ica, 49
Iquitos, 83
Industrial Law 1970, 1, 123–6, 127
Industrial Promotion Law 1959, 25
International Investor, 155
International Monetary Fund, 155
I.M.F. *Survey*, 116, 146
International Petroleum Company (IPC), 3, 14, 23, 34, 43, 48, 53, 54, 57, 74, 78, 87, 88–90, 91–2, 96, 98, 132, 163, 164
International Telephones and Telegraph (ITT), 37

Jiménez de Lucio, Admiral Alberto, 136, 144, 146, 152

Kedourie, 53
Kennedy, John F., 117
Kennedy, Robert F., 67
Klaren, 15, 18, 20, 33, 34
Knight, 105, 141
Kuczynski, 38, 70

Landázuri, Cardinal Bishop of Lima, 80, 91
Latin America, 46, 68, 69, 86, 90, 123, 131, 139, 142, 144, 154, 155, 157
Latin American Economic Review, 158
Latin American Times, 140
Laudo, the, 59; see also International Petroleum Company
Left, the, 4–7, 38–40, 48–9, 58, 145
Leguía, Augusto B. (President 1908–1912, 1919–30), 15, 17
Levingston, 57
Lewis, 58
La Libertad, 123
Lima, 13, 15, 25, 29, 30, 48, 94, 110–111, 136, 146, 156
Linares, General, 81
López Casillas, Air Force General, 84, 85
Loret de Mola, Carlos, 70
Loveday, 17, 19
Lowenthal, 3, 4, 24, 37, 64, 105, 106, 115, 116, 120, 126, 129, 141, 147, 161

Malaga, General, 82
Maldonado Yanez, General Alberto, 80–1, 90–1
Malloy, 129
Malpica, Carlos, 15, 27, 37, 152
March, 106
Marichetti, 57, 81
Marka, 123, 144, 145, 163
Marks, 57, 81
Marxism, 29, 51, 69, 96, 163
McCoy, 37, 38
McNamara, Robert, 81
Mercado Jarrín, General Edgardo 82–3, 85, 92, 94, 136, 138, 151
Meza Cuadra, General Anibal, 85, 92, 93

INDEX

Middlebrook, 122, 130, 131
Miguens, 75, 110
Miller, 4, 19, 33, 36, 120, 121
Mining Law 1950, 24
Mineroperú, 147, 148
Minogue, 53
MIR (Movimiento del Izquierda Revolucionaria), 39
Mirages, 57, 140
Miró Quesada (family), 86; see also *El Comercio*
Miró Quesada, Don Antonio, 20
Miró Quesada, Alejandro, 68
Miró Quesada Bahamonde, Air Force Lt.-Gen. Fernando, 154
Molina, Colonel, 78
Montagne, General Ernesto, 79–80, 82, 85, 90–1, 92, 101, 114, 124, 128
Montero, Air Force Major-General Eduardo, 85, 92
Moquega, 131
Morales Bermúdez, Colonel Fransisco, Governor of Trujillo, 20
Morales Bermúdez, General Fransisco (President 1975–), 72, 73, 92, 93, 101, 114, 124, 136, 137, 138, 151, 153, 154, 155, 157, 158
Moran, 161
Moreira, 76

Navarro, Vice-Admiral Alfonso, 83, 85, 90, 92
Navy, 83–4, 104, 107–11, 138–9, 154, 157
Needler, 11, 75
Neustadt, 10
New York Times, 6, 65, 80, 81, 155, 160
Niera, 28, 35, 38, 83, 139
Noriega Calmet, Senator Fernando, 69
North Korea, 162
Nueva, 152, 153
Nueva Cronica, see *La Cronica*
Nun, 10

Odría, General Manuel (President 1948–56), 13, 21, 22, 28, 29, 30, 32, 33, 34, 35, 36, 40, 41, 54, 71, 76, 79, 83, 85
Oiga, 27, 73, 78, 86, 88, 92, 129, 140, 141, 146, 147, 154
Oligarchy, 5, 6, 14–17, 25–7, 28, 30, 32–3, 50, 52, 78, 97, 132
d'Onis, 57
Opinión Libre, 143, 155
Orrego, 145

Panama Canal, 18
Pardo, President Juan, 15
Pardo de Zela, Admiral, 84
Payne, 44
Peñalosa, Walter, 139
Pérez, Carlos Andres, 156
Pérez Godoy, General (President 1962), 44
Perón, General Juan, 123, 160, 166
Peruvian Association of Oilmen, 61, 63
Peruvian Times, 61, 63, 69, 140, 142, 149
Petras, 124
Petroperú, 112, 147
Philip, 4, 19, 97, 102, 105, 116, 147, 161
Pike, 22
Pinelo, 58, 69, 71, 73, 161
Pinochet, General Augusto, 143
Piura, 82, 131
Pizzorno, 102
Plan Inca, 142
Podestá Jiménez, Air Force Lt.-Gen. César, 154
Poggi, Air Force General Dante, 154
La Porte, 124
Portocarrero, Felipe, 6
Potash, 11
Powell, 29
Prado (family), 23, 26–7, 76, 82, 86, 103, 132
Prado, Manuel (President 1939–45, 1956–62), 30, 34, 35, 36, 40, 53
La Prensa, 33, 60, 61, 62–3, 76, 82, 84, 89, 102, 139; see also Beltrán
Puno, 143

Quechua, 106, 136

INDEX

Quijano, 4, 5, 6

Ra'anan, 11
Ramirez Novoa, Ezequiel, 58, 68, 86, 87
Richter Prada, General Pedro, 144, 152, 154
Right, the, 5–8, 48–9, 85–6
Roberts, 19, 29, 33, 121
Rockefeller, Governor Nelson, 94
Rodríguez Figueroa, General Leonidas, 78, 85, 87, 108, 110, 114, 129, 131, 136, 144, 153–4
Rodríguez Razetto, General, 82
Roemer, 24, 35
Roper, 93
Ruíz Eldredge, Alberto, 68, 86, 87, 89, 91, 139

Sala, Lt.-Gen. Pedro, 138, 144, 152
Sánchez Cerro, Colonel Luis M. (President 1931–33), 17, 20, 33, 71
Sánchez Salazar, Admiral, 81
Santistevan, Carlos, 155
Schurmann, 102
Scott Palmer, 120, 122, 130, 131
Sechura Desert, 71
Segura, General, 140, 144
Seoane, Edgardo, 48
Seoane, Eduardo, 32
Sierra, 14, 27, 49, 117, 119, 120
Simon, 106
Sinamos, 103, 108, 122, 127–31, 135, 143
Smith, 4, 19, 120
Social Progresistas, 49, 68–9; see also Ruíz Eldredge
Social Property, 141–2, 157–8
Sociedad y Politica, 4
Soldi, Air Force General Jorge, 84
Southern Peru Copper Corporation, 24, 36, 147
Stepan, 10, 41
Standard Oil of New Jersey, see International Petroleum Company
Sulmont, 19, 22, 30
SUTEP, 143

Tacna, 110
Talara, 14, 27
Talara, Act of, 70–1, 73, 74, 87, 98; see also International Petroleum Company
Tantaleán, General Javier, 103, 110, 137, 144, 152, 154
Thorndike, Guillermo, 126, 139, 140, 142
Thorp, 3, 17, 25, 26, 115, 126
Toquepala, 24, 36
Treverton, 57, 58
Trotskyists, 39, 138
Trujillo, 21, 157
Tugwell, 161

Ulloa, Manuel, 30, 76, 85
Ultima Hora, 139
Union Nacional Odríista (UNO), 35, 46–8, 65; see also Odría
Uruguay, 163
U.S.A., 19, 31, 55–8, 64, 67, 77, 87, 90, 93–4, 116, 132, 156
U.S. Department of Commerce *Survey*, 116
U.S.S.R., 93, 102, 133, 139
Utley, 97

Valdivia, General Angel, 82, 85, 89, 90–1, 118
Valderrama, 119, 120, 131
Valdéz Angulo, General Enrique, 140
Valdéz Palacio, General, 78, 141
Valdéz Pallete, 41
Vargas, Getúlio, 163, 166
Vargas Caballero, Rear-Admiral Luis, 92–3, 104, 106, 111, 136, 138, 139
Vargas Haya, 47
Vargas Prieto, General, 156
Velarde, León, 86
Velasco, General Juan (President 1968–75), 27, 55, 74, 76–7, 84, 85, 88, 90, 92, 94, 98, 99, 103, 104, 105–6, 107, 108, 109, 110, 111, 113, 115, 123, 128, 134, 136, 140, 144, 151, 152, 158, 162, 166, 167

Villanueva, Armando, 156
Villanueva, Victor, 10, 21, 41, 42, 44, 57

Washington, see U.S.A.
Washington Post, 151, 156
Webb, 115, 126
World Bank, 50, 155

Yepez, Air Force Lt.-Gen. César, 154

Zaire, 162
Zavaleta, General, 144, 152
Zileri, Enrique, 103; see also *Caretas*
Zimmermann, Augusto, 47, 58, 64, 67, 84, 85, 86, 87, 88